COMING EVEN CLEANER ABOUT ORGANIZATIONAL CHANGE

Jerry L. Patterson

A ROWMAN & LITTLEFIELD EDUCATION BOOK
Published in partnership with the
American Association of School Administrators

Rowman & Littlefield Education
Lanham • New York • Toronto • Plymouth, UK

This title was originally published by ScarecrowEducation.
First Rowman & Littlefield Education edition 2006.

A ROWMAN & LITTLEFIELD EDUCATION BOOK
Published in partnership with
the American Association of School Administrators

Published in the United States of America
by Rowman & Littlefield Education
A division of Rowman & Littlefield Publishers, Inc.
A wholly owned subsidary of the Rowman & Littlefield Publishing Group, Inc.
4501 Forbes Boulevard, Suite 200, Lanham, Maryland 20706
www.rowmaneducation.com

Estover Road
Plymouth PL6 7PY
United Kingdom

British Library Cataloguing in Publication Information Available

Library of Congress Cataloging-in-Publication Data

Patterson, Jerry L., 1944–
  Coming even cleaner about organizational change / Jerry L. Patterson.
      p. cm.
  "Published in partnership with the American Association of School
Administrators."
  "A ScarecrowEducation book."
  Includes bibliographical references and index.
  ISBN-13: 978-0-8108-4739-2 (pbk. : alk paper)
  ISBN-10: 0-8108-4739-6 (pbk. : alk paper)
  1. School management and organization—United States. 2. Organizational
change—United States. 3. Educational leadership—United States. I. Title.
LB2805.P327 2003
371.2'00973—dc21

                                                            2003001320

∞™ The paper used in this publication meets the minimum requirements of
American National Standard for Information Sciences—Permanence of Paper
for Printed Library Materials, ANSI/NISO Z39.48-1992.
Manufactured in the United States of America.

This Book is dedicated to the memory of my mother-in-law and dear friend, Shirley Himes. You served as a role model for others in how to bounce back and move ahead in the face of adversity.

CONTENTS

PREFACE

This book stands out from the usual crop of books on leadership, organizational change, and resilience. The centerpiece of the book is a dozen bold, even bald, realities about people and organizations—bold because the realities challenge conventional wisdom about how to lead organizational change; bald because the realities lay bare for public exposure and dialog "things we already know but do not want to talk about." My passion in this book is to help leaders lead others to achieve mutually agreed upon goals, grounded in moral purpose, that take the organization to a higher level in the face of adversity. But my firm belief is that we cannot get there by resurrecting the usual checklist of optimistic, rational strategies deemed necessary to bring about culture change. And we cannot get there by quick fixes. Despite the fact that *Who Moved My Cheese?* was the top-selling business book three years in a row, checklists and quick fixes are recipes for disaster. To illustrate the point, think back on your entire career and try to list examples of culture change that were initiated from *within* your organization, designed to affect the norms and values of the organization, and were successfully implemented for at least six years. How long is your list?

By confronting statements like the one above, you may find this book hazardous to your sense of optimism but, paradoxically, a boost to your sense of hope. Vaclav Havel (1993) defines optimism as the belief that things will turn out as you would like. Hope, on the other hand, is the belief in yourself that causes you to fight for what is right, just, and reasonable irrespective of the outcomes. So when it comes to confronting the harsh realities of leading culture change, this book offers hope.

This book is for you if you are a leader of change initiatives. By applying the concepts and strategies in this book, you increase the batting average of seeing your change initiatives successfully implemented and sustained over time. Throughout the book, I emphasize that leaders are not just those who hold an official leadership title. Some of the most significant examples of leading culture change occur by those of you in teacher leader roles and other informal roles of influence.

This book is for you if you are a manager of change initiatives launched by someone else. Under these conditions, you face the formidable task to make something work that was not your idea in the first place. The concepts and skills described in this book will help you make it work.

This book is for you if you are on the receiving end of change initiatives. As you come to a greater understanding of the harsh realities and the nature of how true culture change happens, you will have a deeper sense of how you can be meaningfully a part of the change you are expected to implement.

Finally, this book is for you if you find yourself in the predicament of having to lead, manage, or implement culture change imposed on you by outside forces. One person's or group's initiative is another person's or group's imposition. Many school leaders like you find that they are so consumed by wrestling with imposed change, they never have the time to lead their own culture change initiatives. In *Coming Even Cleaner about Organizational Change* you will learn how to engage in "and" thinking, that is, how you can work within the reality of an imposed change *and* be true to the values of the change initiatives you hold as an educational leader.

In summary, if you are prepared for honest, candid discussion about things you already know and do not want to talk about, and if you are prepared to apply the concepts in this book to increase the odds of successfully implementing culture change, then be prepared for increased hope that you can do what is right, just, and reasonable irrespective of the outcomes.

❶

NEW WAYS TO THINK ABOUT ORGANIZATIONAL CHANGE, LEADERSHIP, AND RESILIENCE

One thing that sets this book apart from other books about leadership and change is how the concepts of organizational change, leadership, and resilience are defined and applied. The standard textbook approaches to these concepts no longer fit the reality of today's leaders. For example, when groups of leaders are asked to list all the changes that have affected them professionally over the past three years, they fill pages of chart paper. When asked to compare the past with the rate and complexity of change plus the adversities they expect during the next three years, virtually everyone agrees that the rate and complexity of change will increase and adversity will become greater. Therefore, it is more critical than ever for you to understand the complexities of organizational change, your role in successfully guiding an organization through change, and the strategies required to help your organization, as well as yourself, move through change and adversity to greater resilience.

LEVELS OF ORGANIZATIONAL CHANGE

Often the literature on organizational change tends to treat the subject in very broad terms. Underneath the label, however, there are four distinct levels of change, each with its own distinct personality.

Culture Change

The levels of organizational change can be thought of in terms of four concentric circles. As shown in figure 1.1, the inner circle represents culture change. It is no accident that culture change is at the center; it is central to producing long-term, meaningful change in organizations. Culture change is driven by what the organization values and, as amplified in chapter 2, affects virtually everything the organization believes, does, and says.

To effect long-term, meaningful change, you need to focus on culture change. Many attempts at this goal, however, fall short of the mark. For example, numerous schools across the country now claim to operate as middle schools. However, the norms, values, and relationships within some of the schools remain basically unchanged from the junior high model. Adults still view children as *junior* high school students and the

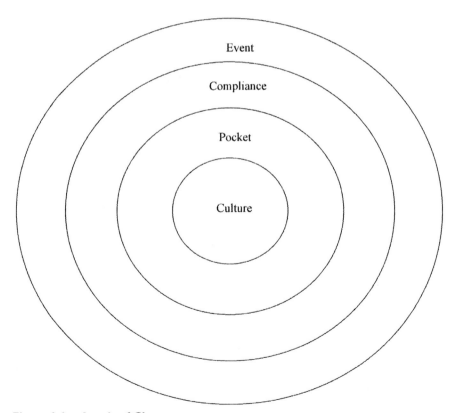

Figure 1.1. Levels of Change

teaching-learning process operates accordingly. Therefore, despite good intentions, culture change has not occurred.

Culture change happens only when the people inside an organization critically examine their fundamental organizational beliefs and change their practices to fit their revised beliefs. For educators in a school or district to truly achieve culture change related to middle school philosophy, they must first believe that students in the middle grades have educational needs that distinguish them from fourth graders and tenth graders. Teachers must then construct learning environments that capitalize on cooperative learning, personalized attention, integrated curriculum across subject areas, and other innovations reflective of the idea that middle school students are not just *junior* high school students. In addition, the relationships within the school must be altered to reflect the new norms and beliefs.

Pocket Change

The next layer of change is pocket change. This level of change affects the cultural norms and beliefs in pockets of the organization, without having a major impact on the total organization. Sometimes pocket change intentionally focuses on selected segments of the school culture. At the elementary level, the Reading Recovery program, which assists first-grade students with severe reading needs, is an illustration of pocket change. The program can be effectively implemented at the primary level, without a significant culture shift throughout the school or school district.

In other instances, pocket change is the result of intended culture change at the school level that never takes hold across the entire school, even though pockets of teachers strongly believe in the underlying values of the change. This situation occurred when the Coalition of Essential Schools was attempting to implement culture change in high schools. The Coalition's reforms were based on nine principles designed to bring about improved teaching and learning at individual school sites that agreed to participate.

The Coalition founders sought schoolwide change. According to the research, what they achieved is far different. In most Coalition schools, no consensus existed agreeing that fundamental changes in school structure or teaching practices needed to occur, even after the schools agreed to participate according to the fundamental beliefs underlying the Coalition's philosophy. Instead, certain pockets of faculty members at most schools became active in their school's reform efforts, but their efforts often ended up dividing the faculty (Muncey and McQuillan 1993).

Compliance Change

The third level of change happens when members of the organization bear the brunt of change initiatives forced on them by outside forces. These so-called outside forces can take the form of the board of education enacting a new policy requiring all students to wear school uniforms. Even though the schools and the community had no input into the rationale behind the policy, all students are expected to comply with the new rules. They are forced to change their conduct, even if they do not support the driving beliefs underlying the required behavioral change. In a similar way, school districts are bombarded by changes being forced upon them by federal and state agencies. The No Child Left Behind (NCLB) legislation championed by the Bush administration in 2002 is a prime example of how school districts are expected to comply with new laws, despite protests from school districts that the laws are based on values that are antithetical to student learning.

Event Change

The outer ring of the concentric circles is event change. This level of change usually has no staying power. In the end, it turns out to be just another event in the life of a school or district with little connection to the core beliefs of the organization. Many attempts at culture change result only in event change. Newly appointed superintendents are notorious for restacking the boxes on the district's organizational chart. They typically have good intentions for their reorganization initiative, but the people occupying the boxes find ways to continue operating in the "business as usual" mode. Similarly, school leaders, determined to show that their schools are not standing still, grab a hot topic like brain-based approaches to assessment and make valiant efforts to implement the reform. However, with the crush of so many competing demands on time, the staff do not have adequate preparation to understand and integrate the beliefs of brain-based approaches to assessment. What starts out as a culture change ends up as just another in a long line of events that happen momentarily and then fade away.

In summary, culture change is what leaders most often strive for in moving the organization to a higher level. This level of change has the greatest long-term impact on what the organization believes, does, and says. Most of the time, however, change initiatives get stuck at the pocket change, compliance change, or event change level, falling short of the hopes of those committed to bringing about culture change in the organization.

EFFECTIVE LEADERSHIP

So much has been written about effective leadership that you may find yourself struggling to decide what to read and whom to believe. I include in this section a summary of some of the best current thinking about core leadership skills.

Goldberg (2000b, 2001) interviewed more than forty leading voices and distilled five qualities of effective leadership from his rich sources of data:

- Bedrock beliefs that inspire you to pursue your work.
- Perseverance to act on your beliefs in the face of criticism and resistance.
- A social conscience to make a contribution to humanity.
- Seriousness of purpose, devoting years of service to your beliefs.
- Ability to match your leadership strengths with the needs of the organization looking for leadership.

Goldberg refers to the above points as five large-minded qualities, not simple-minded answers to the question of what constitutes effective leadership.

Kanter (1999) studied leaders for over twenty-five years and found that the following skills are needed by leaders to move the organization forward:

- Tune into the environment by actively listening to what is happening inside and outside the organization.
- Challenge prevailing organizational wisdom by looking at different ways to interpret the patterns of what is happening.

- Communicate a compelling aspiration by appealing to a cause beyond one's self.
- Build coalitions by determining who holds the resources, knowledge, and political clout to make things happen.
- Enlist others in implementation by supporting the team and providing coaching and support, as well as setting boundaries that define the freedom for others to operate.
- Learn to persevere, realizing that everything looks like a failure in the middle of change.
- Recognize, reward, and celebrate accomplishments by giving credit to all of those who contribute to success.

Kanter believes that leaders set direction and provide coherence for their organization by applying the skills just outlined.

Collins (2001) conducted a five-year research study of leaders who have taken their organizations from "good to great." He found a hierarchy of skills that describe effective leaders, with Level 5 leaders being those who transformed their organizations to greatness. Collins describes two major skill areas that separate the great from the merely good leaders. One skill area he refers to as personal humility, operationally defined as the ability to:

- Demonstrate a compelling modesty, shunning public adulation and never boastful.
- Act with quiet, calm determination, relying on inspired standards (not inspiring charisma) to motivate.
- Channel ambition into the organization, not the individual.
- Look into the mirror, not out the window, to apportion responsibility for poor results.

In tandem with personal humility, the concept of professional will is a second factor uncovered in Collins's research that separates great from good leaders. He defines professional will as the ability to:

- Create superb results.
- Demonstrate an unwavering resolve to do whatever it takes to produce the best long-term results, no matter how difficult.

- Set the standard for building an enduring organization, settling for nothing else.
- Look out the window, not in the mirror, to apportion credit to others for the success of the organization.

Although you will not find a one-to-one correspondence of effective leadership variables across researchers, you will note some common themes: bedrock beliefs about what matters most, perseverance in the face of adversity, passion to contribute to humanity, and determination to give others credit for the organization's success.

Leading versus Managing

Another theme running through most of the research on effective leadership is the distinction between leading and managing. As Kotter (1996, 2001), one of the nation's leadership experts reports, leadership and management are two complementary systems of action. Management is a set of processes that keeps a complicated system of people and technology running smoothly. The most important aspects of management include planning, budgeting, organizing, staffing, controlling, and problem solving. Leadership is a set of processes that are designed to achieve culture change. More specifically, Kotter contends that leadership defines what the future should look like, aligns people with that vision, and inspires them to make it happen in the face of adversity. He also argues that successful culture change is 70 to 90 percent leadership and only 10 to 30 percent management. So even though management and leadership are complementary, for the purposes of leading culture change, leadership becomes most crucial. In making this point, I do not intend to trivialize the management component. In fact, according to a recent study of public school superintendents and principals, a majority of both superintendents and principals said that they are so overwhelmed by day-to-day activities of management that they cannot provide the necessary visionary leadership (Johnson 2002). Acknowledging this reality, I argue that you need to rise to the challenge of learning how to lead culture change as you simultaneously manage the day-to-day affairs of your organization.

Leading with Moral Purpose

Any discussion of effective leadership is incomplete without attention to the dimension of moral purpose. In Fullan's view (2002), moral purpose is social responsibility to others and the environment. Hesselbein (2002) says that the leader of the future will not be the leader who has learned the lessons of *how to do it* but will be the one who has focused on *how to be,* that is, how to develop quality, character, values, principles, and courage driven by moral purpose. The *how-to-be* leader demonstrates core beliefs about the rights, worth, and dignity of humanity. An exemplary document expressing a set of universal values about moral purpose is the United Nations' Universal Declaration of Human Rights. The declaration sets forth thirty articles to serve as a common standard for defining moral purpose for all peoples and all nations. Effective leadership, therefore, is leadership that occurs within a foundation of moral purpose.

The Special Case for Informal Leadership

Even though the research presented in this book primarily emphasizes leaders in formal roles, the concept of effective leadership does not reside exclusively with those sitting in formal seats of authority. Granted, for many years the effective schools' literature argued that if principals directed the work of teachers, held high expectations, and provided caring and support, teachers would produce and principals would be regarded as effective leaders. Today things are different. Today the evidence is clear that teacher leaders within schools, as well as others providing direction from informal leadership roles, contribute a great deal in helping the organization move ahead. As one researcher concludes (Lieberman 1992), teacher participation in leadership may be the most crucial component of the entire process of culture change. So any serious discussion of effective leadership needs to honor the special place that informal leaders have in helping the organization achieve desired goals.

Summary

To condense a vast amount of research on effective leadership into a one-sentence definition: *To lead is to influence others to achieve mutually agreed upon goals, grounded in moral purpose, that help an organization stretch to a higher level in the face of adversity.*

ORGANIZATIONAL RESILIENCE

In the definition of effective leadership that I just presented, I said that leadership, in part, is taking the organization to a higher level in the face of adversity. Adversity is included as part of the leadership equation because virtually all leaders claim, as I commented in the beginning of this chapter, that adversity overwhelms them in their leadership role. They also are quick to acknowledge that adverse conditions are going to get even worse in the future. Therefore, an indispensable element of effective leadership is to take the organization to a higher level, despite adverse conditions. In other words, effective leaders are called upon to build more resilient organizations and more resilient individuals along the journey of building more effective organizations. In this section I outline a framework for understanding resilience.

The Conceptual Framework of Resilience

In summary form, resilience means *moving ahead in the face of adversity.* However, like many other sensationalized topics that grab public attention for brief periods then vanish, the topic of resilience runs the risk of overuse, abuse, and disappearing. Therefore, to avoid the resilience slogan falling victim to the forecast, "this too shall pass," and to sharpen the focus in studying the construct, I strongly believe that school leaders, as well as researchers, need to be explicit and clear about the concepts contained within the label. This can be achieved by asking two questions. (This section is adapted from my research reported in *Bouncing Back! How Your School Can Succeed in the Face of Adversity* [Patterson, Patterson, and Collins 2002].)

Question 1: What is the target level we want to hit in achieving resilience?

Based on our research (Patterson et al. 2002), resilience gets interpreted in various ways. Specifically, resilience can be viewed as having three possible *target* levels. Depending on your view of the concept, people or organizations can be characterized as being resilient if they are (1) just getting by, (2) getting back to the status quo after experiencing adversity, or (3) getting ahead through consistent improvement or consistently high performance.

To illustrate the point, imagine that three schools across the nation recently experienced the tragedy of a school shooting. Emerson High School takes this approach, "Our goal is to survive this crisis without the community coming apart at the seams." The school operates in survival mode, continually struggling with its grief. Morale remains low as Emerson High School struggles to hold itself together.

East High School, facing a similar crisis, commits itself to returning to "normal" as a target. The goal is for the school to overcome adversity by restoring the school culture to the condition before the crisis.

Poindexter High School embraces a different orientation. Learning from the pain of the crisis, they believe they can eventually be even stronger than they were before the events occurred. The Poindexter staff and community set their sights on moving ahead, not surviving or merely getting back to the status quo.

Understanding the target level you hold is central for school leaders committed to resilience. In my view, and as documented by substantial research, the only long-term perspective that reflects the deepest meaning of resilience is the perspective of *moving ahead*.

Question 2: What is the condition of our adverse environment?

In most of the research on resilience in educational settings, adverse school environments are characterized as either ongoing adversity or crisis adversity. To contrast the two environments, consider two different school examples.

Dade Middle School, set in the middle of one of the poorest housing projects in this large city, starts each day with adversity oozing from the pores of the school. Poor facilities, poor economic conditions, and poor community support combine to constantly challenge the Dade staff and students on a daily basis. Everest Middle School recently absorbed the shock of the sudden loss of twenty students and three teachers when a chartered school bus on the way to a football game slid down a steep embankment. The entire Everest community struggles to get out from under the pain of this crisis adversity.

In this book, I focus on the target level of moving ahead within the context of both crisis and ongoing adversity. In other words, this book is about leadership strategies that help schools effectively answer the question: "How can we use our energy productively to move ahead in the face of crisis or ongoing adversity?"

The Importance of Resilience Capacity

Now that I have erected the scaffolding for understanding the concept of resilience, I need to also elaborate on the power of resilience capacity. Imagine for instance that your school, creatively named *School A,* has a resilience capacity today depicted in figure 1.2. This capacity represents the "resilience points" your school has in its tank to move ahead in the face of adversity. Down the road from you is School B, which has a comparable resilience capacity. In other words, both schools today are poised with equal resilience to face the future.

However, as the future unfolds, certain dynamics kick in. Your school makes a conscious effort to implement strategies to help your entire staff become more resilient. You search for strategies that minimize the amount of resilience points you have to spend on any adversity you face. For example, you learn not to be surprised, and waste resilience points, when disruptions to your expectations pop up. You also seize the opportunity to

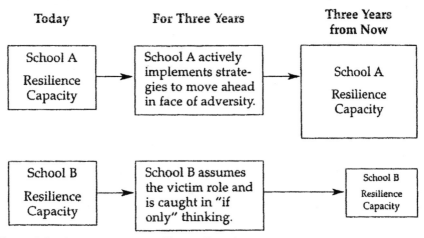

Figure 1.2.   Importance of Resilience Capacity

grow your resilience capacity by strengthening your skills to handle disruptions when they do occur. So you minimize the amount of resilience taken out of your resilience account when adversity happens and you maximize the amount of resilience you add to your account by adding more skills to your repertoire.

Your colleagues down the road in School B take a different approach. They face adversity with the proverbial "if only" thinking. You can almost hear the principal telling the staff, "We could do what is important to us if only those outside the school would quit placing so many new demands on us." By putting themselves in the dependent, victim status of not being responsible for their own organizational health, they place themselves at the mercy of others and continue to deplete their resilience account.

Three years later, your school and School B are ready to face the future. However, each of you is positioned to face future adversity with fundamentally different resilience capacities. As shown in figure 1.2, your resilience capacity has grown dramatically because of the steps you have taken. Unfortunately, because of the approach taken by School B toward adversity, they will be tackling the future with a drained resilience account. Imagine the cumulative impact of these dynamics over time. Also imagine the school you would prefer to be associated with over time.

Your leadership role is to continually look for ways to help those within the organizational culture strengthen the skills needed to adapt to change and thus remain resilient during change. To successfully fulfill this role, you need a framework for understanding and assessing the organizational culture you are leading. I construct this framework in chapter 2.

2

A LEADER'S GUIDE
TO UNDERSTANDING
ORGANIZATIONAL CULTURE

Organizational culture is a concept that is elusive to find and slippery to hold. Even with these somewhat mysterious qualities, organizational culture may be the most powerful construct that you as a school leader can use to bring about change. As Fullan put it: "Reculturing is the name of the game. Transforming culture, changing what people in the organization value and how they work together to accomplish it, leads to lasting change" (2002:18). Barth (2002) takes the argument farther by asserting that a school's culture has more influence on life and learning in the school than the president of the country, the state department of education, or any of the school district's senior administrators. Correspondingly, he argues that culture change is the most difficult and the most important job of the instructional leader. So if culture change is the name of the game and if culture is so hard to get a handle on, where do school leaders start? One place you can start is by reading this chapter. In the following sections, I provide a comprehensive framework (adapted from Schein 1999b) to guide you through a culture review of your organization. The steps in the culture review involve asking the following questions: (1) What are the ingredients of your culture? (2) What is the current reality of your culture? (3) What is the health of your organizational culture? (4) What is needed to strengthen the health of your culture?

WHAT ARE THE INGREDIENTS
OF ORGANIZATIONAL CULTURE

Imagine you walk into my kitchen and see on the counter a container of espresso coffee, a partial bottle of rum, a carton of eggs, a sugar bowl, a salt shaker, some cheese, several packages of ladyfinger biscuits, and cocoa powder. You surmise that I am getting ready to prepare some concoction, but, at this point, you are not sure what this strange assortment of ingredients is intended to produce. In a similar way, the "production" of organizational culture begins with the raw material of certain sets of ingredients. In this section, I describe the most essential ingredients of organizational culture: culture anchor-points, culture questions, and culture content.

Culture Anchor-Points

The dynamics of organizational culture, illustrated in figure 2.1, grow out of the interaction among three anchor-points: (1) Believe (what you truly believe), (2) Do (what you actually do), and (3) Say (what you say you believe and what you say you do).

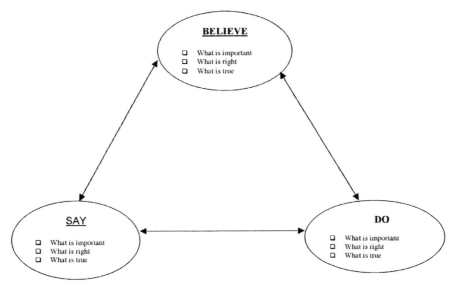

Figure 2.1.   The Dynamics of Organizational Culture

What you truly believe refers specifically to the beliefs about what is important, right, and true that have given your organization shape and substance over time. These beliefs are tacit assumptions that are not readily evident to those outside the organization. In fact, the assumptions may not be easily recognized or articulated by those inside the organization. However, regardless of their degree of visibility, true beliefs do indeed drive what you do in the organization. So the ability to uncover and describe these beliefs is a critical ingredient in understanding and assessing the dynamics of organizational culture.

What you actually do reflects all tangible evidence of your culture being enacted on the stage of real life. Your artifacts and documents, your use of resources such as space, time, and money, as well as your treatment of each other inside and outside the organization all encapsulate what you *do* as an organization to express what you believe.

What you say you believe and what you say you do is what you espouse. In other words, this dimension of organizational culture reflects what you talk about regarding your actions and beliefs. In reality, what you say may show a strong relationship to what you believe and do. Or, in some cases, there may be poor alignment between what is said and what is actually done or truly believed.

To review, the culture anchor-points of Believe, Do, and Say form the first set of ingredients for organizational culture. Standing alone, they add little meaning until you mix in another set of ingredients, three culture questions that take you to a deeper understanding of what culture is all about.

Culture Questions

The culture question, *What is important?* refers to what you hold as organizational values. Core organizational values typically have their roots in the organizational mission. Illustrations of core values found in our nation's schools include:

- We value improving student learning.
- We value providing a safe, supportive environment for learning to occur.
- We value high expectations that all students will achieve at or above the standards we establish.

By asking what is important to your organization, you target what matters most among all the competing demands for your time and your commitment. Much of the attention in the professional literature to core organizational values is, in effect, attention to the culture question of *what is important?*

What is right? refers to general ethical virtues of right and wrong, irrespective of the particular mission and type of organization. Examples of ethical virtues are:

- We value acting with integrity in all that we do.
- We value acting in a trustworthy manner.
- We value treating each other with dignity and respect.

In one sense, ethical virtues can be considered a special case of organizational values. However, generally the purpose of organizational values is to express what is important relative to the nature of the organization's reason for being. What is right transcends purpose and focuses on more universal, timeless virtues.

The third culture question, *What is true?* addresses what you assume to be reality about the world, or at least the part of the world that pertains to your organization. Sample statements of what a school district may consider to be reality are:

- All students can learn.
- Adults in the workplace want to be seen as caring and competent.
- When faced with imposed change, people think first of their own self-interest, not in the interests of the organization imposing the change.

As you ask questions about what is true, you are not usually focusing on divine truth as revealed through religious doctrine. Primarily, you are asking questions about reality that affect what you believe, do, and say in your organizational culture.

Up to this point, I have outlined two kinds of ingredients that go into the mix of organizational culture: culture anchor-points and culture questions. When you lace these components together, you achieve the following type of question related specifically to your organization:

What do we *believe* (culture anchor-point) is *important* (culture question category)? At this juncture, you still do not know what you are asking questions about. The last batch of raw material making up culture is the ingredient of culture content.

Culture Content

Culture content is the "stuff" of organizational culture. In conducting a culture review, both the reviewers and organization being reviewed should know what content areas (identified below) of the organization are central to more fully understanding the concept of organizational culture.

The culture content related to *what is right* can be found in what your organization ethically values. For instance, does your organization prize honesty, trust, integrity, compassion, diversity, and morality? Are there other ethical virtues that your organization believes in? Although there are no predetermined universal virtues that each organization must embrace, every organizational culture does in fact respond to *what is right* in ways that reflect what the organization believes about right and wrong.

The culture content contained in the question about *what is important* can be gleaned from data in a variety of areas, including organizational identity, means to achieve the identity, means to measure success, communications processes, power and authority, relationships, rewards and punishment, and resources. I will briefly describe how each of these dimensions contributes to the raw material of culture content.

In the case of organizational identity, a culture review looks at, for instance, what people truly believe about the future direction of the organization, what they say about how the organization should look five years from now, and what they do to act in ways that help make the vision become reality. As an illustration, what is your organization doing in the areas of employee recruitment, induction, and development? What are the organizational structures, policies, and procedures in place to support your identity? By asking questions such as these, you develop a deeper understanding of your organizational culture.

Understanding how you achieve your identity is a necessary, but not sufficient, condition to understand what is important to your organization. You also need to know how you measure success. So you ask questions to produce culture content about outcome measures of success, strategies for analyzing outcome data, as well as strategies for making changes based on any discrepancies between actual performance and expected performance. These data provide insights into the *how* of getting to your goals.

Understanding your organization's formal and informal communication process is another major ingredient in making sense of organizational culture. If you know how the organization communicates information, decisions, and organizational values, you have a sense of what is important. Keep in mind that these cultural norms of communication are dictated in large part by the power brokers of the organization. Some of the power brokers sit in positions of authority, so it is important in a culture review to know who they are. Oftentimes, though, the informal power structure plays an even bigger role in shaping organizational conscience about what is important. Find out where the power is, and you find out a lot about the culture.

Organizational relationships are important in two distinct ways in connection to culture. First, how your organizational members treat each other on a daily basis, both in small workgroups and within the total organization, speaks volumes about what matters most. Second, how your organization views conflict as a phenomenon and how you handle conflict when it rears its ugly head shapes culture over time. The stories that get passed through the organization and passed down by the informal gatekeepers of history signal what the organizational culture stands for in the area of relationships.

If you want to understand the dynamics of culture, you should pay particular attention to the culture content of rewards and punishment. The well-worn saying still applies today: what you measure determines what people attend to. Virtually every organization has formal performance appraisal policies and procedures in place. Does the formal system reflect what supervisors actually judge to be important? And, on an informal basis, are there any patterns regarding who gets rewarded and punished and what types of behavior get rewarded and punished? What does all of this information signify about culture?

Some of the strongest messages sent about organizational culture come in the form of messages about which resources are most important. During so-called flush times, organizational priorities about the relative importance of various resources can be somewhat hidden.

There is plenty to go around, and everyone benefits. More often, though, the supply of resources does not match the heavy demand, so some things get more attention than others. Under these conditions, what areas get the most attention? How are space, equipment, and supplies allocated? The answers to these and other questions convey what is really important in the organization, as well as who is really important. Finally, what are the norms at work regarding organizational time as a resource. You can learn a lot about organizational culture when you learn how time is used and how its value is reflected in relation to meetings and individual appointments.

The culture content for the third culture question, *what is true,* draws heavily from what the organization assumes to be true about human nature, employees, and those outside the organization. By using all of your sensory data to discern what the organization believes to be true about human nature, you gain insights into how the organization treats the humans who work there. If you know what the organization thinks about those they serve, you have an added glimpse into organizational reality. You can also determine a lot about culture when you uncover how the organization views reality in relation to the outside world. For instance, does the organization see itself as a victim of external forces? Or does it see itself as the primary shaper of its own culture? Answers to these questions provide insight into what the organization considers to be the reality of the world in which it operates.

The ingredients of culture anchor-points and culture questions combine with the culture content ingredients highlighted in this section to produce material that can be used as a "Culture Review Guide." Below I offer a sample guide. I should point out, however, that these questions are indeed only samples. Depending on the nature of an organization and the specific dimension of culture being examined, questions can be added, changed, or dropped.

Culture Review Guide
Culture Question: What Is Right?
Our Virtues

Ethics
  • What are our ethical principles about right and wrong?

Culture Question: What Is Important?
Our Identity

Mission
- What is our fundamental reason for existing?

Vision
- What do we want to look like five, ten years from now?
- What are our central goals to propel us toward our vision?

Organizational Values
- What are our core organizational values that provide the foundation for our mission and vision?

Means to Achieve Our Identity

Employee Recruitment
- What are our recruitment policies and practices?

Employee Induction
- What are our employee induction policies and practices?

Employee Development
- What are our employee development policies and practices?

Structure
- What is our formal organizational chart?

Policies
- What are our official policies that guide our work?

Procedures
- How do we organize our human resources to deliver our work?

Means to Measure Success

Outcomes
- What are our measures of success in meeting student and adult goals?

Data Analysis
- What are our strategies for collecting and analyzing data relative to achieving our goals?

Data-Driven Adjustments
- What do we do when we find that our actual performance does not meet our expected outcomes?

Communication Processes

Formal Communication
- What are the primary ways we formally communicate information, decisions, and what we value?

Informal Communication
- What are the primary ways we informally communicate information, decisions, and what we value?

Power and Authority

Power
- What is the informal power structure operating in our organization?

Authority
- What is the formal authority structure of supervision?

Relationships

Interpersonal Interactions
- How do we treat each other within our smaller work groups?
- How do we treat each other within the larger organization?

Conflict
- How do we view conflict within the organization?
- How do we handle conflict among peers and between supervisors and subordinates?

Rewards and Punishment

Rewards
- What does our formal performance appraisal system look like?
- What types of behavior does our organization reward?
- What forms do organizational rewards take?
- What signals do we pay attention to in determining what gets rewarded?

Punishment
- What does our formal reprimand and punishment system look like?
- What types of behavior does our organization punish?

- What forms does organizational punishment take?
- What signals do we pay attention to in determining what gets punished?

Resources

Financial
- What are our priority areas in the expenditure of funds?
- How are our priorities determined?

Time
- What are the priority areas in how organizational time is spent?
- What norms does our organization have about time related to group meetings and individual appointments?
- What norms does our organization have about amount of time expected in a typical work week?

Space
- What gets priority attention in how the organization allocates space?
- How does the organization express rank and status in the allocation of space?

Equipment and Supplies
- What gets priority attention in how the organization allocates equipment and supplies?
- How does the organization express rank and status in the allocation of equipment and supplies?

Culture Question: What Is True?
Assumptions about Reality

Human Nature
- What are the dominant assumptions our organization believes to be true about human nature?

Customers
- What are the dominant assumptions our organization believes to be true about those we serve?

Employees
- What are the dominant assumptions our organization believes to be true about our employees?

Those in Authority
- What are the dominant assumptions our organization believes about those in authority positions?

Climate
- What is the current organizational climate like in the organization?

External Forces
- What are the dominant assumptions about the impact of external forces on our organization?

WHAT IS THE CURRENT REALITY OF YOUR CULTURE?

Up to this point, I have offered an explanation of the ingredients that comprise the raw material of organizational culture, that is, culture anchor-points, culture questions, and culture content. But the raw material is not the culture. It is the ingredients that come together in dynamic fashion to produce a reality far more significant than the sum of the parts. To illustrate the message, let's return to my kitchen. Recall, on my counter sits some raw material, including espresso coffee, rum, and eggs. Now let's mix them together in the following very methodical way.

In a medium size bowl, mix espresso with rum. Set aside. Separate the eggs. In a small mixing bowl, beat egg yolks and sugar until thick and fluffy. Set aside. In a large bowl beat the egg whites and salt until whites are airy and creamy. Add the yellow mixture to the white mixture. Add the cheese and mix well. Dip the ladyfinger biscuits lightly in the coffee/rum mixture. Layer cream mixture on top of ladyfingers; sprinkle with cocoa. Repeat the process of ladyfingers, cream, and cocoa. Chill for about four hours. Then hang around to enjoy the product, *tiramisu.*

Similar to the process just described, when it comes to producing the reality of organizational culture, we mix the raw material of Believe, Do, and Say with the questions about what is right, what is important, and what is true. Finally, we stir in enough culture content to give the other ingredients sufficient substance. The outcome is a dynamic produced by how all of the raw material relate to each other. Probably the most significant relationship within organizational culture occurs in how the three anchor-points relate each other. I will examine, in turn, each of the three sets of relationships: say ↔ do, say ↔ believe, and believe ↔ do.

A major factor shaping organizational culture is the relationship between what the organization says it does and what it actually does. To use a specific example related to the culture question *what is right,* suppose a high school staff says that they believe it is right for adults in the school to treat *all students* with dignity and respect. Now imagine that an outside team conducting a culture review observes that the following conduct is typical behavior by the staff. Athletes are put on a pedestal and success in athletics is more valued than success in academic achievement. Students with disabilities are housed in a separate wing in the school. Students who are transported to the school from an impoverished neighborhood are referred to as the "have-nots." Therefore, the culture review team records their observations about the relationship between what the adults say they value about treating all students with dignity and respect and what they actually do on a day-to-day basis within the school culture.

Another key component of organizational culture is the connection between what people say they believe and what they actually covet as deeply held beliefs. Suppose that a middle school faculty says they value meeting the very special academic and social needs of the adolescent. Suppose, further, that the school has fully implemented the middle school model, including interdisciplinary teams, advisor–advisee concept, exploratory learning, and afterschool clubs. Anyone who observes the school in action can see the positive relationship between what is said about middle school beliefs and what is really believed.

The third relationship occurs between what people actually believe and what they actually do. To illustrate the relationship between actual beliefs and actual conduct, consider a university school of education that takes special pride in how they recruit, mentor, and develop the faculty. The odds are high that the organizational culture reflects some very visible things to demonstrate the strong belief system. They use all available tools and informal contacts to identify the most promising candidates. The school of education invests heavily in providing a multiyear induction program for newly hired faculty. Also, the administration establishes professional development as a priority item in the budget. Finally, the teaching faculty feel pressure from their peers to stay on top of the most current research and best practices in their academic areas. In other words, there is ample evidence to determine the relationship between what the school of education faculty truly believe and what they actually do.

WHAT IS THE HEALTH OF YOUR ORGANIZATIONAL CULTURE?

Although a description of current reality about your organizational culture helps to develop a picture of what is really going on, the investment of time, energy, and other resources to develop a comprehensive picture of organizational culture must have a payoff other than a developed picture. Organizational leaders need to be able to judge the relative health of the organization. This is accomplished by starting with a simple query: *To what extent does the organizational culture demonstrate alignment among the dimensions of Believe, Do, and Say for each of the culture questions?* This initial query generates a more extensive set of questions to gauge the status of organizational health:

- What is the degree of alignment between what we say we do and what we really do in the areas of what is right, what is important, and what is true?
- What is the degree of alignment between what we say we believe and what we actually believe in the areas of what is right, what is important, and what is true?
- What is the degree of alignment between what we actually believe and what we actually do in the areas of what is right, what is important, and what is true?

As you can see, these specific questions about alignment yield rich data to determine the health of your organization. Among the alignment patterns, I contend that the *believe ↔ do* relationship is most critical. I said earlier that organizational beliefs about what is important, right, and true drive how the organization behaves over time. So if the organization conducts itself in concert with what it genuinely believes, by definition there is strong alignment and, I would submit, a healthy culture.

WHAT IS NEEDED TO STRENGTHEN THE HEALTH OF YOUR CULTURE?

After you understand the current reality of your culture and you have a firm grasp on the level of alignment among the various relationships, next decide what needs to be done to reconcile any areas of misalignment. For instance, if what you actually do relative to employee development is not aligned with what you really believe is important about employee development, then first determine the source of misalignment. Many times, the problem can be traced to what I call *cultural drift*. Even with the best of intentions, organizations find that their conduct has a tendency to drift away from what they really value. Your own organization can take deliberate steps to remain alert to cultural drift. For example, periodically gather data internally by asking, "How are we measuring up relative to what we say is important and what we actually do?" Invite outside teams into your organization to help you spot cultural drift so you can make midcourse corrections in your conduct to achieve better alignment. On rare occasions, the data showing misalignment may flag the fact that your organization has changed what it values over time and that the core values are what need realigning.

Once decisions are made about what needs to be done, the last step is rather straightforward. Develop an action plan to address the areas where misalignment is most significant, keeping in mind that no organization operates in perfect alignment all of the time. In other words, do not be too hard on yourself as an organization if the culture review fails to report total alignment. Just decide where concentrated action is needed, if at all, and move ahead.

FINAL CONSIDERATIONS

In this chapter, I have provided you with a comprehensive framework to guide you through a culture review of your organization. Before you begin your actual journey, though, let me offer four points to keep in mind along the way. First, the review does not have to necessarily be a review of the total organizational culture. It is absolutely acceptable, and many times more productive, to conduct a culture review of a particular program area or change initiative. On the one hand, a new superintendent may have a strong need to understand, from a school system perspective, the alignment of the overall organizational culture. On the other hand, a new elementary principal may choose to focus on understanding the dynamics of organizational culture related to the school's mathematics program. Some questions that a school may ask to gain a cultural perspective of what is really going on in mathematics are:

- What do we want our math program to look like five years from now?
- What are the core organizational values of our math program that provide the foundation for our mission and vision?
- How do we organize our human resources to deliver our work in our math program?
- What are the primary ways we formally communicate information, decisions, and what we value related to our math program?
- How do we view conflict within our math program staff?
- What signals do we pay attention to in determining what gets rewarded in our math program?

These questions provide a flavor of how a culture review can meaningfully focus on one aspect of the organization's program. Simply apply all of the concepts developed in this chapter to any initiative that is grounded in values and assumptions about how the organization should function.

A second point to keep in mind when you engage in a culture review is deciding in advance *who* should conduct the culture review. Generally, it is unwise to have someone immersed in the life of the organization play an active role in conducting the culture review. Any member of a culture has difficulty disassociating his or her own view of the culture from how others may see the culture. This issue gets more complicated when it comes to making judgments about the health of the culture.

Third, those involved in the review should be on the lookout for distinctive subcultures within the dominant culture. Depending on the size of your total organization, you may have at least three subcultures: the senior management subculture, the middle management subculture, and the frontline subculture. In the case of school districts, the superintendent and senior administrators may operate within a common cultural worldview, the principals may hold a shared organizational worldview, and the teachers may operate with a cultural perspective that is particular to them. Any time a culture review is conducted, when you start asking questions about what people believe, do, and say, make sure your data collection process includes the ability to sort information by subcultures.

A final key point to consider is the data collection strategy. Although Cameron and Quinn (1999) claim to have valid, reliable written instruments to measure organizational culture, other researchers such as Schein (1999b) contend that organizational culture is a group relationship phenomenon, and, therefore, any measure of culture must occur within a group setting. I strongly argue in favor of the Schein perspective. Particularly when the conceptual framework is built on the dynamic relationships among what is said, actually done, and truly believed, accurate data depend on observations of group dynamics and observations of organizational conduct.

Organizational culture is alive in your organization, affecting everything you believe, do, and say. Given the power of culture to affect your long-term organizational health, you need to periodically take stock of your organization through a culture review process. In this chapter, I have provided a comprehensive framework to guide you through such a process. This culture review involves collecting data to gain an understanding of "what is really going on around here," using the data to make a diagnosis of your organizational health, and taking the necessary culture change steps to sustain a healthy culture in the future. It is vital, however, that you do not take these steps without a solid understanding of the harsh realities about how people individually and organizational cultures as a whole respond to culture change. Chapters 3 and 4 of this book examine a dozen harsh realities about people and organizations.

3

HARSH REALITIES ABOUT PEOPLE

Historically, school leaders have proceeded with the best of intentions to lead successful culture change and build resilient organizations. Unfortunately, they have often operated from the following misguided, though attractive, assumptions when trying to effect change:

- People act first in the best interests of the organization.
- People want to understand the *what* and *why* of organizational change.
- People engage in change because of the merits of the change.
- People opt to be architects of the change affecting them.
- Organizations are rationally functioning systems.
- Organizations are wired to assimilate culture change.
- Organizations operate from a value-driven orientation.
- Organizations can effect long-term culture change even with short-term leadership.
- Organizations can achieve culture change without creating conflict in the system.

Operating from these faulty assumptions, leaders have applied faulty strategies and, therefore, unintentionally created a huge drain on organizational resilience as they fail at implementing culture change.

In chapters 3 and 4, I propose a different way of thinking about leadership in organizations. Specifically, I examine a dozen harsh realities about people as the basis for leading culture change and creating more resilient organizations:

Realities about people:

1. Most people act first in their own self-interest, not in the interests of the organization.
2. Most people do not want to genuinely understand the *what* and *why* of organizational change.
3. Most people engage in organizational change because of their own pain, not because of the merits of the change.
4. Most people expect to be viewed as trustworthy, even though they view with mistrust the motives of those initiating organizational change.
5. Most people opt to be victims of change rather than architects of change.

Realities about organizations:

6. Most organizations operate nonrationally rather than rationally.
7. Most organizations are wired to protect the status quo.
8. Most organizations initiate change with an event-driven mentality rather than a value-driven mentality.
9. Most organizations engage in long-term change with short-term leadership.
10. Most organizations expect the greatest amount of change with the least amount of conflict.

Realities about people and organizations:

11. Most people and organizations deny that the other ten realities are, in fact, their own reality.
12. Most people and organizations *do* have the capacity to develop resilience in the face of the other eleven realities.

Most people reading the list for the first time find it intriguing but a bit unsettling. After further contemplation, however, school leaders across the globe have not only confirmed the list as an accurate description of reality in educational organizations but have expressed appreciation and relief that, as one school principal said to me, "The truth has finally been told in these dirty dozen harsh realities. Now we can quit pretending that people and organizations function in rational, organizationally benevolent ways. Now we can face the truth and see how we can work within it to provide top-notch leadership."

The harsh realities fall into the category of what I call "Things we already know, but don't want to talk about." Over time, you accumulate a database about reality related to individuals and organizations. Many times, you find that the reality you have discovered is not one you hoped to find. So you tuck your discovery way back in the recesses of your mind, pretending it does not exist. In the short run, this strategy is less disruptive to your own way of making sense of the world. In the long run, though, things you already know but do not want to talk about have a away of resurfacing and wreaking havoc with your false sense of how things really are. So, as unsettling as it may be in the short run, now is the time to talk about these unsettling things you already know. Now is the time to openly discuss them so you can develop leadership strategies to move ahead in the face of the harsh realities.

As you confront these "dirty dozen" harsh realities, it is important to remember that each of the realities is intended to reflect a generalization about *most people* or *most organizations*. Clearly, you can think of people—you and me, for instance—who are exceptions to each statement on the list. Your natural tendency, then, is to argue that because of the exceptions you can so readily recite, the statements are not valid. For instance, suppose a small elementary school in the Midwest is able to achieve culture change in how they teach reading. People need to celebrate the success of the school's accomplishments. At the same time, the harsh realities remain valid as generalizations and have been documented by nearly four decades of serious study about educational change, including that by Fullan (1991, 2002), Goodlad (1984), and Sarason (1996). Denying these realities because you know of exceptions is simply making an excuse for not doing some of the difficult things you must do to effect change.

If you are truly interested in helping your organization stretch to new heights, you must examine each of these realities, determine how each plays out in your own organization, and implement leadership strategies that allow you to use the tensions created by each as a fulcrum for leveraging change.

Before I begin to examine each of the harsh realities about people, I need to clarify that the leadership strategies I discuss are built on the assumption that the change initiative is initiated from within the organization. As complicated as it is to lead self-initiated change, life for leaders gets even more complicated when change is imposed on the system. In chapter 6, I specifically address leadership in the face of imposed change. For now, however, let's turn to how you can lead change that you support in face of realities that are sometimes less than supportive.

REALITY #1: MOST PEOPLE ACT FIRST IN THEIR OWN SELF-INTEREST, NOT IN THE INTERESTS OF THE ORGANIZATION

When people feel the winds of change blowing across an organization, the natural response is to say, "What's in it for me? How will I benefit? Why should I change?" The nature of these concerns has been documented by Hall and colleagues (Hall and Hord 2001, Hall and Loucks 1978), who found that people respond predictably to proposed organizational change. First, they want to know, at a surface level, what the change is about. Next, they move to the personal stage of concern and demand to know how this so-called change will affect them and their professional space. And third comes what Hall calls the management stage of concern, which is characterized by questions such as, "How can I possibly fit this into a crowded workday?" and "What will I have to give up that I currently like in order to manage this change?" The researchers found that generally people express primary concerns about the interests of the organization only *after* they satisfactorily resolve their self-interests. And some people never move beyond the personal and management stages of concern.

As the targets of culture change, it is human nature for people to think first of themselves. Acting first out of self-interest does not mean people are selfish or disloyal to the organization. It reflects people's need to conserve their scarce resilience points. People cannot afford to automatically rally around every change initiative anyone inside or outside the organization dreams up. To maintain any sense of resilience in the face of change, individuals must spend their energy on initiatives that have a payoff for them.

Reality #1 in Action

In an urban southern high school, a group of teachers becomes increasingly concerned about the poor academic performance by many of the students. The teachers are convinced that students will perform better if they have the benefit of smaller groups of students working closely with a small cadre of teachers. So the teachers submit a request to attend a three-day conference on small learning communities (SLC). Upon their return, the teachers march into the principal's office, present their case for starting the SLC concept the next semester, and ask for time on the next faculty agenda to present their findings. Reluctantly, the principal agrees.

At the faculty meeting, the SLC advocates request a chance to form a study committee and return to the faculty within ninety days. Their request is met with a mixture of concern and apathy. However, no one actually speaks out against the idea, so a committee is formed. Curiously, the committee is made up primarily of administrators, the conference group, and English and social studies teachers.

As far as most faculty members know, the topic lay dormant for ninety days. Then it abruptly resurfaces when the committee addresses the faculty with two recommendations: to pilot the SLC concept during the upcoming school year and to implement the concept across all subject areas within two years. The recommendations are supported by plenty of evidence from the literature on SLC, as well as personal testimony from committee members where small learning communities were thriving.

Needless to say, a sleeping giant awakes, nicknamed *self-interest.* People in the math department cannot see how their interests will be served; such a plan would not allow the math teachers to continue teaching the same subjects they have taught for years. The assistant principal in charge of scheduling claims that she cannot possibly make it work. People who teach elective courses worry that they cannot offer the electives to each of the learning communities formed. In summary, the faculty members who were not part of the excitement of developing the SLC concept ask questions such as: "What's wrong with the way we do things now? How is this going to affect me and my department? How can I possibly manage this with everything else the school demands from my time right now?"

After much frustration and many hurt feelings, the principal calls for a vote on the committee's recommendations. Not surprisingly, the group's recommendations suffer a resounding defeat.

Leadership Implications

While the natural tendency of individuals is to act in their own self-interest, the logical tendency of you as a change leader is to sell change on the basis of how good it will be for the organization. You assume that if you can rationally build a case for change based on the benefits to the organization, people rationally will embrace the change and everyone will win. In the small learning communities scenario, committee members flooded the meeting with handouts, charts, articles, and testimonials on the merits of SLC. They presented a rational case. However, the audience members were not in a rational mood. They were in an emotional mood.

Instead of building a compelling case for how a school or school system will be better off, spend much more time up front understanding the self-interests of the people in the organization. Returning to the SLC example, at the committee level, questions such as the following need to be asked: What will each department lose under the SLC concept? How will the plan negatively affect the offering of elective courses? What kinds of headaches will this concept create for the people responsible for scheduling? Who else will be affected by the change? To help address questions such as these, Hall and Hord have developed over a twenty-five year period research-based techniques to measure and monitor the stages of concern that people move through as they struggle to implement culture change. In their recent book, *Implementing Change* (Hall and Hord 2001), the researchers provided extensive examples as well as strategies to assist you as change leader in successful implementation of your change initiative.

Once issues of self-interest are acknowledged and carefully considered, avoid the trap of "either/or" thinking by adopting "and" thinking. In other words, instead of thinking that either the math department gets its way or the committee gets its way, the question needs to be: How can we meet the needs of the math department and also achieve what we need on behalf of the entire school?

By thoroughly understanding how self-interest affects planning for change, you can present the organization's case for change in such a way that individuals understand how their self-interests can be met at the same time the organization's interests are fulfilled. Even though the mere thought of addressing the spectrum of individual self-interests found in an organization might seem overwhelming, denial of this reality creates barriers to change that are much more insurmountable.

REALITY #2: MOST PEOPLE DO NOT WANT TO GENUINELY UNDERSTAND THE *WHAT* AND *WHY* OF ORGANIZATIONAL CHANGE

On the surface, this reality does not make much sense. Why would anyone *not* want to understand a proposed change that could affect him or her? The answer is intriguing and reinforces Reality #1.

Assume, first, that you as an initiator of change have legitimate, compelling reasons for the need to change. Also assume that you do a compelling job of presenting the case for change. In other words, the evidence is conclusive; the need to change is inescapable. If people in the organization acknowledge that the reasons are compelling and that they fully understand them, then they are left with few compelling reasons not to change. So, given people's natural inclination not to want to change, how can they publicly escape the power of reason when privately they seek the status quo? They simply profess to not understand. For example, as long as principals do not quite understand what the superintendent is talking about, they do not have any obligations to buy into a proposed change. Logically, it would not make sense to ask principals to support something that still seems ambiguous or confusing to them. So the people who are the targets of change make sure the responsibility for

achieving thorough understanding about the change rests exclusively
with the change initiator.

Reality #2 in Action

The newly appointed superintendent of an urban district on the East
Coast inherits a very traditional central office organizational structure.
She finds that the system is top-heavy with central office specialists. After several months of careful observations, the superintendent concludes that people throughout the organization have learned over time
to become dependent on the central office specialists. In other words,
social studies teachers are encouraged by the central office to defend
the territory of social studies. Teachers of the talented and gifted are
urged to think only in terms of teaching those who have been labeled accordingly. The supervisor of talented and gifted staff even conveys to
those he supervises that if his position is eliminated, there will be no one
left in the central office to advocate for them or for their students.

The superintendent has a different idea about the role of central office staff. She believes that central office staff members should serve as
generalists, offering direct support to teachers by providing information
and resources to help all teachers. She believes that the current vertical
organizational structure reinforces a too narrow view of subject areas as
the basis for organizing teaching and learning. She also knows that two
years earlier, the school board approved a position paper for the district
that called for an instructional emphasis on core values of integrated instruction across subject areas, plus thematic curriculum incorporating
cooperative teaching and learning. Given this position, the superintendent develops her own concept paper centered on two questions: How
can we best use the talent in central office to reinforce our beliefs about
multidisciplinary curriculum and instruction? And how can we become
instructional generalists instead of subject area specialists, especially
given that our classroom teachers are specialists already?

The superintendent distributes the concept paper at an all-administrators
meeting, spends about an hour outlining her position, then asks for group
questions. Aside from two rather benign questions, the group is silent. The
superintendent interprets the lack of questions to mean that people at least
understand the concepts in the paper, though she knows that not everyone

supports the idea. Once the meeting is over, the central office staff privately start to organize their teachers. In meetings quickly called by the subject area supervisors, the basic response is to claim complete confusion over this new concept and to search for the plan's possible weaknesses rather than its strengths. We do not understand where this plan came from. We do not understand how it will work. We do not understand who will supervise subject area teachers if subject area supervisors have to do something else. We do not understand what will happen to academic standards if academic supervisory positions disappear from the organizational chart. We do not understand how we can hire quality subject area teachers if subject area supervisors do not make those decisions. In short, we just do not understand!

In addition to the private meetings, large contingents of subject area teachers begin bombarding board members publicly with the same questions. At one board meeting, teachers fill the auditorium and, for nearly two hours during the public comment session, demand answers to a barrage of questions they fire at anyone who will listen. Those who reject the central office changes repeatedly implore the board not to accept the superintendent's recommendations until everyone affected has a thorough understanding of the issues raised. In short, people say they would change if, and only if, they thoroughly understood how this newly hatched idea would affect them and help their students.

Leadership Implications

Employees professing to not understand is both a systems issue and an individual issue. From a systems perspective, sometimes you may fail to recognize the distinctions between *receiving, understanding, and comprehending* communication. You can convey information and employees can receive it without any real understanding taking place. For example, a principal can distribute to all teachers an article on brain research applied to classroom management. The principal expects to have a rich discussion on the topic at the next faculty meeting. The teachers, however, do not really understand some of the technical terms and the scientific research cited in the article. Effective understanding has yet to occur. So the principal needs to design strategies and forums to strengthen understanding of the words people received. Comprehension does not occur until employees attach *personal* meaning to the leader's message and the impact of it on their own lives. The principal needs to invest ample time helping the teachers understand the content of the article, as well as the implications for their classroom practice. Generally, at some earlier point, the principal went through the same struggle to move from just receiving the information to understanding and then comprehending the meaning and impact behind the words. The principal must provide leadership to assist the teachers in their own struggle to truly comprehend.

As you work hard to implement culture change, be aware of communication gaps in the system. It is often difficult to trace where the communication channels break down. In our example scenario, subject area teachers received the message sent by the superintendent as filtered through the lens of the subject area supervisors. The intended meaning of the message was most likely altered when interpreted by the supervisors. In other words, you cannot count on the official communications hierarchy to carry accurate and understandable information, particularly about new change initiatives. You must assume a personal responsibility to help identify and close any gaps in the communication process. When you ask recipients of the message the areas where they have inadequate understanding, you can begin to trace where the official communication channels failed to deliver, and you can make adjustments accordingly.

Another leadership implication stems from the issue of burden of proof. Individuals reason that as long as the system fails to communicate anticipated changes and accompanying expectations, they cannot be held responsible for fulfilling the expectations. To overcome the major burden of proving that organizational change was effectively communicated, as a change initiator you must shift significant responsibility for comprehending back to those receiving the information about change. The superintendent in our example scenario, after extensive efforts in using multiple forms and forums for communication, should have conveyed very directly to the supervisors that ample time and effort had been expended describing the proposed change and that the time had come for those who still did not understand to individually declare what they did not understand and what they needed in order to reach full understanding. This request for what people still need from the system should provide the superintendent with insights about the gaps in understanding throughout the organization, so that appropriate strategies can be designed to close those gaps.

The superintendent also needed to clearly state that, at some point, it became patently unacceptable for supervisors to not know what issues were still unclear to them. And as a final step, the superintendent should have assigned a timeline for the confused supervisors to assume responsibility for closing the gaps in understanding and should have explained that failure to do so would be considered a performance issue. Imagine, for example, that the superintendent spent about nine months working through the issues supervisors had about reorganization. Finally, after exhaustive attempts at effective communication, the superintendent met with the supervisors and gave them a sheet of paper containing the following questions:

- What are you still unclear about related to the reorganization plan?
- What support, information, and resources do you need from the system to help you become more clear?

At the bottom of the sheet of paper the superintendent asked for name and signature. Then the superintendent told the group that she would respond to the written information provided. Finally, she commented, "And, six months from now, given what we have done to clarify the confusion, if you still are unclear, then you need to know that we have a performance problem on your part to deal with." As strident as the words from the superintendent may sound, there comes a point in the efforts by you to achieve effective communication that accountability for comprehending has to shift to the receiver of the change, including the possibility of a negative performance evaluation.

By acknowledging people's natural tendency to profess confusion about change, you can implement strategies to ensure that everyone has the necessary information and time to fully understand the *whats* and *whys* associated with proposed change.

REALITY #3: MOST PEOPLE ENGAGE IN ORGANIZATIONAL CHANGE BECAUSE OF THEIR OWN PAIN, NOT BECAUSE OF THE MERITS OF THE CHANGE

In a rational world, people change because it is the right thing to do. So when you initially encounter resistance to your proposed change, you try talking louder, longer, and with more conviction to sell the audience on the merits of the change and the fact that it is the right thing to do. Unfortunately, you are selling the wrong thing.

A significant majority of individuals will not embrace culture change based on its merits but, rather, because of their own pain (Conner 1992; Kotter 1996; Schein 1999a). In other words, individuals need more than to hear a strong argument for the merits of change; they need to weigh the pain of changing against the pain of clinging to the status quo. The pain of clinging to the status quo can take the form of a missed opportunity, a problem left unresolved, or a dilemma not effectively managed. To raise the pain issue to the conscious level, people need to confront a series of questions: What will our organizational life be like five years from now if we continue to do business as usual? How painful will it be? What will life be like if we do accept the proposed changes? Will the short-term pain of changing be less than the long-term pain of holding on to how we currently do business? Candid responses to these questions help people understand how a proposed change, even with the inevitable discomfort, will be worth the effort.

Reality #3 in Action

As part of the No Child Left Behind (NCLB) legislation, suppose the federal government created opportunities for school districts to submit a proposal for teacher recruitment and retention programs. The school board in one rural southern district knows that a successful proposal could generate approximately $100,000, which could be used to train newly hired teachers in areas such as classroom management and lesson planning. Given the high turnover of new teachers leaving for more lucrative jobs, the superintendent realizes this training is something the district desperately needs to provide. But there is a problem. The school board is conservative and will strongly resist any innovation that is not clearly proven to work. On at least three occasions during the past year, the board has rejected various proposals from the superintendent to recruit and retain new teachers. The board argued each time that the money should be spent on higher priorities. Though conditions have changed because the money will not have to come from the district budget, the superintendent still fears that the school board will decide not to apply for the funding.

The superintendent decides to try a different approach than he has tried previously when arguing the case for teacher recruitment. Instead of using his typical rational approach of showing the board data about how teacher recruitment and retention strategies will produce a more stable teaching force in the future, he writes a lengthy memo to the board a week before the monthly meeting. In it, he acknowledges the reasons board members have previously given for not launching a teacher recruitment and retention initiative. But then he asks each board member to ponder the following series of questions: What are the chances we can find $100,000 in our own budget within the next five years to attract and train teachers new to our district? How will you explain to those who elected you that you passed up an opportunity to secure funds that may not come along again? What will you say to the Rotary Club next Tuesday about why you turned down possible funds during a period of scarcity in the district?

When the NCLB funding item comes up for discussion at the board meeting, each board member launches into a little speech about why now *is* the time for the district to make extra efforts to lure prospective teachers into the district. Each speech is a somewhat feeble attempt by the board members to show that they have suddenly seen the need for aggressively trying to secure and keep the "best and brightest" new teachers. In reality, the board's change of heart came about because the superintendent made it clear to the board members that the pain associated with accepting the funds would be less than the pain they would experience when having to explain, at election time, why they passed up the opportunity to apply for $100,000 in "free" money.

Leadership Implications

When it comes to leading culture change, resist the natural temptation to sell proposed change using rational discourse. Instead, sell the need to change by exposing the pain that will result from not changing. One strategy you can use is to help people see the urgency for change, or what Tichy and Charan (1995) call "the burning platform theory of change." Your job is to help people see that the platform is burning, whether the flames are visible or not. As one prominent researcher on organizational change warns, "By far the biggest mistake people make when trying to change organizations is to plunge ahead without establishing a high enough urgency in fellow managers and employees" (Kotter 1996:4). He even goes so far as to say that such an error, the failure to establish a sense of urgency, is likely to be fatal to the initiative's chance of success. He then offers insights about why even "smart individuals" fail to create a sense of urgency at the beginning of a transformation:

- They overestimate how much they can force big changes on an organization.
- They underestimate how hard it is to drive people out of their comfort zones.
- They do not recognize how their own actions can inadvertently reinforce the status quo.
- They lack patience.
- They become paralyzed by the downside possibilities associated with moving people from the status quo.

A leader's platform of urgency can take the form of an opportunity that needs to be seized *now,* a problem that needs to be solved *now,* or a dilemma that needs to be managed *now.* If the situation represents an opportunity to be seized, you can help members of the organization realize the price to be paid for inaction. In the NCLB scenario, the superintendent abandoned his usual approach of selling the issue from a logical, rational perspective. Instead, he created a burning platform, a sense of urgency for securing the funds. He also appealed to the "personal pain perspective" by helping board members see how voters might react at election time to their refusal to take advantage of a small window of a funding opportunity that may never come along again. In other words, he exposed the pain that would result from a missed opportunity.

When the pressing condition is a chance to resolve a burning platform organizational problem, make sure others have the information and tools to understand the long-term pain of failing to rid the organization of a nagging irritation and thereby letting a current problem grow bigger. For example, a school district can control expenses in the short run by not making needed repairs to schools. After about ten years of so-called cost controls, though, the district will face a facilities crisis that is literally out of control. The leader's job is to keep this big-picture perspective in plain sight.

Occasionally you find yourself asking the organization to make a culture change for the purpose of damage control. Such change does not appear to do anything to advance the organization toward a better future, but it does reduce the organizational energy spent on controlling an issue. When the organization is spending too much time messing with dilemmas that, by definition, do not have satisfactory answers, you face the challenge of convincing employees that the implications of bringing about change will be worth the price of changing. If employees realize that leaving the dilemma unmanaged will be a constant pain for them, usually they will consent to spend the energy necessary to keep things somewhat under control. For instance, a school staff might not prefer to waste precious time developing a crisis management plan for the unlikely threat to their school's safety. However, after witnessing the national horrific tragedy of September 11, 2001, virtually any school would now agree that the dilemma posed by managing any kind of threat calls for a concerted schoolwide effort to construct such a plan. As a school leader, a major task you face is to help others see the need to act before a crisis arises.

To summarize the leadership strategies associated with creating a sense of urgency, Kotter (2002) offers advice about what works and what does not work. What works:

- Showing others the need for urgent change with a compelling object that they can actually see, touch, and feel.
- Showing people valid and dramatic evidence from outside the organization that demonstrates that urgent action is required.
- Never underestimating how much complacency, fear, and anger exists, even in good organizations.

What does not work:

- Focusing exclusively on building a rational case, getting top leaders' approval, and racing ahead while mostly ignoring all the feelings that are blocking change.
- Ignoring a lack of urgency and jumping immediately to creating a vision and strategy.
- Thinking that you can do little if you are not the head person.

But what happens when, despite your best efforts, employees still do not see the need to change? Should you move away from the issue, hoping to revisit the topic when the timing is better? Or should you press ahead with changes in the face of massive resistance? According to Heifetz and colleagues (Heifetz and Laurie 1997; Heifetz and Linsky 2002b), the answer can be found in two familiar words: *it depends.* It depends primarily on the stakes involved. If the organization's survival as a productive system is at stake, you must weigh the price paid now by employees versus the price paid later by a dying organization. Under such circumstances, moving ahead now with the changes is clearly in the best long-range interests of the organization.

If the proposed organizational change means changing frameworks, or paradigms, about how the organization should do business in the future, the burden of proof still will be on your shoulders. Most employee groups are not convinced of the need to jump from today's way of doing business to some untested, ill-defined approach tomorrow. And the harsh reality is that logic alone does not work. According to Schlechty (1993), certain groups will not want to change. Those comfortable with the status quo, the "settlers," have no reason to disrupt what apparently is working for them. And the "saboteurs" believe they have every reason to disrupt whatever is being proposed. Only the risk takers, the group Schlechty calls the "pioneers and explorers," are ready to make the leap of faith. So you can turn loose those ready to go and count on the others to make the changes as they see the evidence of success accumulating or push the stragglers out of the nest and expect them to catch up with those who are blazing the trail. Either way, the organization pays a price for expecting people to change. You have to decide whether it is worth it.

If the proposed changes are just improvements in how the organization does business within the current framework, forced change may not be worth the price paid. Instead, you may need to rely on time, logic, and teachable moments to help employees move along the continuum of improvement within the system's current way of doing business.

REALITY #4: MOST PEOPLE WANT TO BE VIEWED AS TRUSTWORTHY, EVEN THOUGH THEY VIEW WITH MISTRUST THE MOTIVES OF THOSE INITIATING ORGANIZATIONAL CHANGE

The first half of this reality seems so obvious. Of course people expect to be viewed as trustworthy. Rarely do we encounter people who say to others (or even to themselves), "What I am about to do is driven by my being untrustworthy." We all view ourselves and expect others to view us as being trustworthy. On the flip side, how many times within your own organization have you heard the following accusations about initiators of change: Do you think we should trust them? What's *really* behind this talk of so-called change? Given what has happened in the past, why should we trust them this time?

So, as ironic as it might seem, when organizational culture change is proposed, "trustworthy" people who are the targets of change tend to question the trustworthiness of those proposing the change. This does not happen with all people and it does not happen all of the time, but the harsh reality is that it happens enough to fan the fires of organizational mistrust. And when organizational mistrust of change erupts, the "trustworthy" targets of change dump the burden of proof into the laps of initiators. Consequently, you as initiator are thrust into the awkward position of proving the trustworthiness of your intentions and struggling to earn the trust of those being asked to change. Note that even more irony gets woven into this mess because the targets of change, the so-called trustworthy ones in a given situation, likely have been initiators of change in another context and, therefore, have been viewed with mistrust.

Reality #4 in Action

A new superintendent is appointed in a progressive midwestern community of about nine thousand students. He comes with the reputation of being a change agent. People are watching him carefully. During the summer administrative retreat before the opening of school, the superintendent speaks openly about his image as someone who likes to shake things up. He reassures his new administrative colleagues that he will not initiate any significant changes during his first two years in office; his primary goal is to become familiar with the culture of the school district and to invite anyone, anytime to discuss with him whatever is on the person's mind. "But," he says, "speaking of change, how many of you as principals have been in your same assignment for more than six years?" Seven of ten hands go up. The superintendent smiles but makes no comment.

About a month later, an elementary school principal takes the superintendent up on his offer to talk. The principal, a high-energy and very progressive thinking individual, says she is getting restless in her position.

She has been in the same job for seven years. She thoroughly enjoys her staff and the community is supportive, but she feels as if she is not growing and inquires about a lateral transfer to another elementary school that will open the following year. The superintendent makes no commitments but indicates he will give serious consideration to her request.

Three weeks later, another elementary principal becomes seriously ill and takes early retirement. The position is filled temporarily by the assistant principal. So, by October, the superintendent is faced with the situation for the following year of having a principalship vacancy in a new school, another vacancy due to illness, and a talented principal who wants a change. The superintendent knows that some action needs to be taken, but he is not sure exactly what that action ought to be. He discusses the situation with the school board president and confides in one of the middle school principals about the possibility of shifting principals. The principal says she thinks the shifts would be viewed as refreshing.

Over winter break, the superintendent looks at the needs of the schools plus the strengths of the principals and devises a very sensible plan. At the January principals meeting, he presents his plan in writing and asks for reactions. He gets what he asks for, but not what he expected. The vocal principals let him know he has violated their trust. They let him know that the word is out that he has been talking secretly with a principal about his scheme to move principals around. They remind him of his promise not to make significant change during the first two years, and they ask why he did not let them know as soon as he began contemplating the shakeup. One veteran principal even comments that it is pretty clear why he has the reputation of being a change agent.

Leadership Implications

As a leader of change, attacks on your trustworthiness can hurt deeply, and several reactions are common. Launch a counterattack. Deny the accusations. Demand concrete proof of the basis for the accusations. All of these reactions are, indeed, natural but they are usually counterproductive. Instead, invest your energy in a positive way by strengthening trust at two levels: interpersonal trust and organizational trust.

One way to strengthen interpersonal trust is through authentic, frequent, even intentionally redundant communication. For example, forecast any possibilities of culture change on the horizon and show how such change directly connects to the bedrock organizational values. There is a natural tendency for you to assume that if you tell others once (or even twice) about a possible culture change, then effective communication happened. The reality, however, is that people need to hear a message several times, sometimes in different ways, before they move from receiving the information to genuinely comprehending the full meaning within the words.

Also, you need to be sensitive to another fact. Just because you make well-intended offers of an open-door policy, many times people are reluctant to accept the offer. Granted that sometimes the reluctance is driven by Reality #2. People do not want to really know the what and why of the leader's culture change ideas. Other times, though, people on the receiving end of change feel vulnerable to engage in candid, open communication with leaders who can affect their future. Farson (1996) contends that this happens because there is not a balance of power. The less powerful feel more vulnerable to the exercise of power over them by others. You can help counteract this concern by first promising that the messenger will not be shot. And then by delivering on this promise when bad news arrives.

Another communication skill that you can use to build trust is to demonstrate sincere listening to what is being said. Think of occasions when you made yourself vulnerable to your supervisor by providing feedback as requested. As you were providing the feedback, you could tell that the supervisor did not really want to hear what you had to say. Often such behavior is not a matter of bad intentions. When leaders invite open communication, they find themselves getting information that causes them to question how they think and feel. This creates internal disequilibrium for them. Keep this in mind when you wear the leader cap. You build trust by authentically listening to what people have to say and treating the feedback with the respect in which it was given. In fact, Farson (1996) says that listening is not so much a set of technical skills as being genuinely interested in what really matters to another person.

In addition to the skills of effective communication, you must be able to examine how your own conduct affects trust within a relationship. Fisher and Brown (1988) encourage you to think about whether you have possibly given others reason to mistrust by asking yourself the following tough questions about your behavior.

Has my conduct been in any way erratic? Even with the best of intentions, sometimes changed circumstances will cause you to do things that you, yourself, could not have predicted. In the scenario above, the superintendent truly did not intend to make any changes during his first two years in office. However, changed circumstances in personnel caused him to prepare a plan of administrative reassignment. Even though in his own mind he resolved the apparent contradiction between what he said to the administrators and what he planned on doing, in the minds of others a serious contradiction existed in what he said he believed and what he actually planned to do. The superintendent could have avoided the perception of erratic behavior by talking with the administrators about his preliminary ideas as soon as possible and definitely before he unveiled any plans for reorganization.

Did I communicate carelessly? Given the numerous meetings you attend with groups who have very specific agendas and pointed questions, it is entirely possible to make statements without careful thought to the weight the audience places on them. You sometimes give your best estimate of a situation while the receivers of the message interpret the comments as a definitive answer. The superintendent presented a plan, fully intending to make changes to the plan based on feedback from the administrators. But the administrators placed considerable weight on the fact that the plan had already been drawn up and written down, with names attached to the administrative moves. In their view, he had violated what he promised, while in his view he just communicated carelessly.

Did I treat a promise or commitment lightly? In the scenario, the superintendent did say he would not initiate significant changes for two years. However, he did not think it was any serious breach of trust to change his mind. As he put it to a superintendent in another district, "I don't see what the big deal is." From the perspective of trust, the big deal in the eyes of the administrators was that the superintendent was messing with their professional lives. They took his promise very seriously.

Did I actually deceive others? Many times, you want to spare others the pain of worrying needlessly about proposed change. So when teachers ask a principal whether there has been discussion about cuts in teacher positions at the school next year, the principal may give an ambiguous reply when, in fact, the superintendent had met just the night before with the principal and informed him or her confidentially that the school would lose two teachers due to a shift in student enrollment. Unfortunately, a little bit of dishonesty or deception creates a lot of mistrust. And it hangs around for a long time.

When you find yourself in the predicament of having to answer "yes" to one or more of the above questions, you must be forthright with the answer and pledge to be more vigilant about your behavior in the future. You can put yourself in a trustworthy position if you honor the following public commitment to everyone: *I will do what I say I will do when I say I will do it. And, because I am human, there will be (hopefully) only rare instances when I violate my commitment. In those cases, you have an obligation to tell me immediately, and I have an obligation to demonstrate that it will not happen again.*

If you measure trust by your track record of doing what you say you will do when you say you will do it, there is hope for changing people's perceptions about the intentions of your actions. Over time, you must establish a track record of repeatedly carrying out, in full view of the organization, the meaning of trust so that others can see the track record being set and comfortably conclude that your intentions are as trustworthy as their own.

Along with strengthening interpersonal trust, you must increase trust people have in the system. And people already know what trustworthy systems look like. To illustrate the point, try this exercise (Farson 1996). Ask people to design an organization that would produce the lowest levels of trust among its employees. In other words, what actions would they take and what policies would they put in place to create a low-trust organization. At this point, people start to realize they are describing aspects of their own organization. Then reverse the exercise. Ask people to invent a high-trust organization, based on the idea that human nature is not all that bad. According to Farson, people tend to generate maxims that sound very much like what is typically taught as good leadership practices today. "In short, what flows naturally from a belief in the positive side of human nature is just sound management, and the positive approach can become just as self-fulfilling as the negative" (1996:131).

An example of these principles in practice is building into the organization a system of justice that allows people to challenge the conduct or intentions of those at the top of the organizational chart without fear of retribution. Apart from the typically adversarial grievance process, you can create a system that allows teachers, administrators, and other employees to discuss issues surrounding trust in a safe environment. For example, one school district has an Issues Resolution Council for each employee group. On a regular basis, the superintendent meets with representatives of the employee groups to discuss issues or concerns that might be brewing related to mistrust between the employee group and senior management. Over time, leaders can demonstrate that they are serious about wanting to build stronger relationships and open to challenges about their own leadership behavior. In the school district using the Issues Resolution Council concept, the number of formal teacher grievances dropped dramatically over a five-year period. People welcomed an alternative to the formal grievance procedures, knowing they always had the formal process if they needed it.

In another district, the superintendent convened an advisory panel of employees across all employee groups. The exclusive purpose of the group was, as the superintendent phrased it, "To tell me things I don't want to hear. Tell me what I need to know, even if it makes me uncomfortable with how I am conducting myself as a leader." The group met four times a year. The superintendent provided feedback in writing on how she was addressing each item presented. She also made deliberate efforts to show her respect for the risks people took in telling her bad news, including not blaming any of the individuals personally for the messages that were delivered.

By strengthening interpersonal and organizational trust, you are more likely to be viewed as having good intentions by those whom you are asking to undertake culture change.

REALITY #5: MOST PEOPLE OPT TO BE VICTIMS OF CHANGE RATHER THAN ARCHITECTS OF CHANGE

The literature on educational leadership is replete with calls for employee involvement. Leaders are advised to give employees considerable autonomy in constructing how proposed change initiatives will affect them. Leaders are not advised, however, about what happens next.

Employees have a tendency to turn their backs on autonomy and circle their wagons around dependency.

As paradoxical as it may seem, people have a love–hate relationship with autonomy (Block 1987). On one hand, employees sincerely claim they want to be architects of change that affects them. On the other hand, they fall into the dependency trap of wanting someone to nurture them, someone to care for them, and someone to blame (Conner 1992). Autonomy carries with it responsibility, which translates into being held accountable for one's own action. Dependency carries with it a patriarchal contract, which translates into being protected by those above . . . as long as one does what he or she is told. Given the history of organizations encouraging the patriarchal contract, it is *natural* for employees to choose the safety of being dependent victims of change. It is *unnatural* for them to choose the ambiguity and risk inherent in being held accountable as architects shaping how change affects them.

Reality #5 in Action

An elementary school principal has been in her assignment for three years. During the first year, she used the former principal's system of scheduling the art, music, and physical education classes. The system was not complicated; the principal did all the work. After the first year, however, the schedule met with a chorus of complaints. Primary teachers complained that they did not have common planning time for reading. A fifth-grade teacher objected to having all of her planning time in the afternoon. Another classroom teacher said it was not fair that one of the principal's so-called favorite teachers had had planning time right before lunch two years in a row And the kindergarten teachers pointed out that they were the only ones who did not have at least one break a day. Even the teachers of art, music, and physical education began complaining.

When scheduling time occurred the next year, the principal promised to fix the areas of concern and proceeded to single-handedly build the schedule again. And they complained again. In year three of scheduling, the principal refused to unilaterally build the schedule and appointed a committee to work on it. But instead of completing the master schedule, the teachers completed a grievance form against the principal for requiring them to do administrative work.

Leadership Implications

The reality of people choosing to be victims rather than architects of change does not mean people are bad, lazy, or uncaring about their organizations. As Oshry (1992) argues, it is as if people are standing in front of two doors: Door A and Door B. Door A is the victim door, and behind it is a powerful force pulling us through without deliberative thought or conscious choice on our part. Behind Door B, the architect door, is a brick wall. If we choose Door B, we actually have to create our own opening. It is not the natural, easy choice to make.

Because people often think and act based on their worst fears of what can happen, they remain trapped in the victim status. They lose any sense of control over their future. This sense of loss is captured in the parable *Who Moved My Cheese* (Johnson 1998). As I discussed in Reality #3, you are charged with creating burning platforms that force people to jump from their comfortable perches. But this strategy can backfire if it creates panic that stops forward movement. So you must be attuned to where people are relative to their individual zones of performance. In figure 3.1, I show three different "zones of performance" people can occupy when faced with proposed culture change. Even within a given zone, people can be at various levels of performance. Below I apply this concept to a hypothetical school situation involving primary teachers and their reading program.

In the center is the *Comfort Zone,* the preferred place to be for virtually everyone as they seek harmony in their professional workspace. Within the *Comfort Zone,* the "quiet level" is the peaceful spot where no disturbances are heard. This is where things are humming in the classroom and the usual routine proceeds without interruption. Certain teachers at the school get moved to the "disquiet level" when particular noises in the office environment mildly disturb the quiet space. Disquiet occurs, in this scenario, when the principal hints that "given our students' scores at the primary level, perhaps we need to take a closer look at our reading program." At either level within the *Comfort Zone,* employees' work productivity remains relatively undisturbed.

Disturbance first starts to show up when people are pushed into the *Discomfort Zone.* In this area, teachers develop heightened attention to what could happen if a new reading program affects how they teach reading. The level of "productive discomfort" is where people are most effec-

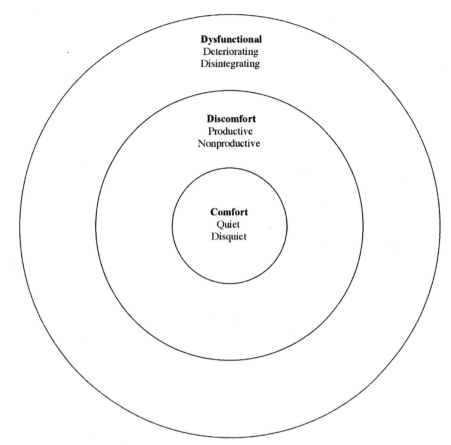

Figure 3.1.   Zones of Individual Performance

tive in confronting the sources of discomfort and using their energy to move through the discomfort to a higher level of growth. Related directly to the proposed culture change of significantly changing the reading program, people in the area of productive discomfort draw energy from realizing that the old way of doing business does not quite fit and that they can help shape the new way by becoming active in examining new textbooks on the market and new strategies to address student diversity. They realize that the discomfort cannot be wished away by them. If growth is to occur, they know they need to acknowledge that the discomfort is real and then use the energy generated from productive discomfort to make the culture change work for them, not against them. Other teachers find themselves being pushed too far out of the comfort zone, landing at the level of *nonproductive discomfort.* At this level, the ambiguity surrounding potential changes in the reading program leaves some individuals too paralyzed to take positive action. They cannot effectively do their everyday work because they worry about an uncertain future where they may forced to teach in ways that are beyond their ability level.

The victim role I referred to earlier starts to show up in the *Dysfunctional Zone.* At best, in this zone people operate at the "deteriorating level" where fear resides. If it becomes clear to some individuals that they are too far behind the current research and best practices to ever catch up, understandably productivity starts to deteriorate and many people react to the culture change by adopting the victim role. At worst, within the *Dysfunctional Zone,* some people are pushed to the "disintegrating level" where their dysfunction is manifest in behavior such as totally shutting down or quitting their job altogether.

The leadership implications of understanding the Zones of Performance are significant. To most effectively achieve culture change, you need to push people out of their comfort zone and into the level of productive discomfort. At this level, they are able to effectively use the energy of their discomfort to meet the challenges posed by the culture change. If you push too hard, too fast, you can push people beyond their zone of productivity into the dysfunctional zone, where they adopt the victim role. When this happens, it becomes resilience draining for everybody, the initiators and the implementers, to try to return them to the level of productive discomfort.

Sometimes you unintentionally contribute to others' victim status by reinforcing the patriarchal contract. You encourage the parent–child status between yourself and employees. You take care of those you supervise in exchange for total loyalty. In the elementary school example about class schedules, the principal unilaterally built the schedule, unilaterally tried to fix the problems, and then in year three unilaterally told others to fix it themselves. To create more healthy organizations, your challenge is to break the dependency spiral. The break begins when you create a climate that dissolves the patriarchal, parent–child relationship and replaces it with an environment that honors employees as equally valued members of the organization. Once such a climate is established, employees feel safer taking the risks associated with being architects of change.

The break also occurs when you help others see there is no silver bullet that external forces will produce. When people choose to become less dependent on external answers, they give up looking for solutions in the wrong places. According to Fullan, "Giving up the futile search for the silver bullet is the basic precondition for overcoming dependency and for beginning to take actions that do matter. It frees educational leaders to gain truly new insights that can inform and guide their actions toward greater success, mobilizing resources for teaching and learning with children as the beneficiaries" (1998:8).

When people think and act based on their highest hopes for the future, they find new energy and creative possibilities. These contrasting orientations between motivated by worst fears and highest hopes are not just matters of strategies. They are fundamental differences in how people choose to frame their ways of thinking about organizations. The choices people make have a direct affect on their resilience. You can help clarify that these choices exist. And you can provide support, information, and resources to help people successfully make the more painful choice to go through Door B and embrace both the responsibility and accountability of being architects of change.

4

HARSH REALITIES ABOUT ORGANIZATIONS

In the previous chapter, I focused on examining selected harsh realities about how people think and act as they confront possible culture change. For each of the harsh realities about people, keep in mind that individuals vary in their adaptation to change. For example, some people will move quickly through the self-interest stages of concern in order to get to the stages of concern related to student achievement (Hall and Hord 2001). Other individuals stay stuck, as the characters in *Who Moved My Cheese?* in the self-interest stages. So on one hand, you have a responsibility to pay attention to the individuals affected by the culture change. On the other hand, you have to pay close attention to the group as an organizational culture. Even though individuals understandably are located at different points of productivity and comfort when faced with change, there is a dominant culture of norms and values that plays a heavy role in the success or failure of change. In this chapter, I address harsh realities that pertain to the organization as a cultural phenomenon and the leadership implications of working within these organizational realities.

CHAPTER 4

REALITY #6: MOST ORGANIZATIONS OPERATE NONRATIONALLY RATHER THAN RATIONALLY

To fully understand the power of this reality we must first develop a common understanding of the concepts of rational and nonrational organizations (Bolman and Deal 1997; Patterson, Purkey, and Parker 1986). Related to organizational life, figure 4.1 contrasts rational and nonrational perspectives for understanding how organizations tend to function. Briefly stated, rational systems function with a single set of uniform goals that provides stable, consistent direction to the organization over time. The power to make things happen resides almost exclusively at the top of the organizational chart. In fact, the formal chart determines who can

	Rational	Nonrational
Goals	• There is a single set of uniform goals that provides consistent direction for us. • The district goals are clearly stated and specific. • The goals remain stable over a sustained period of time. • Organizational goals are set via a logical, problem-solving process. • The goals for the district are determined by the leaders of the organization.	• There are multiple, sometimes competing sets of goals that attempt to provide direction for us. • The district goals are somewhat ambiguous and general in nature. • The goals change as conditions change. • Organizational goals are arrived at through bargaining and compromise. • The goals for the district are set by many different forces, both inside and outside of the organization.
Power	• The formal organizational chart determines who can have power to make things happen. • Power to make things happen is located almost exclusively at the top of the organizational chart. • There is a very direct connection between what the central office says should happen in the classroom and what actually goes on behind the classroom door.	• Having access to information, support, and resources is the basis for power to make things happen. • Power to make things happen is located throughout the organization. • The extent of implementing central office directives is in large part controlled by teachers at the classroom level.

Figure 4.1.   Rational and Nonrational Models Contrasted

Continued

Decision Making	• The issues that receive attention are those that are most important at a given point in time. • The decision-making process makes sure that all feasible options are considered. • The decision-making process keeps away extraneous forces (e.g., competing demands, outside pressures) that negatively affect logical decision making.	• The issues that receive attention are those that are pressing for immediate resolution. • The decision-making process usually ends up with a limited number of options to consider, constrained by factors such as politics, economics, and finances. • The decision-making process accommodates various forces shaping eventual decisions (e.g., external pressures and persistence of people in their points of view). • The decision-making process incorporates compromise and concession, leading to a decision that may not have been the most educationally sound decision.
External Enviroment	• The environment external to the school district remains passive while organizational decisions are made internally. • The external environment acts in a stable and predictable fashion. • The external environment respects and defers to the official expertise and official power vested in school district staff. • The external environment acknowledges the right of the organization to make its own decisions.	• The external environment maintains an active level of involvement in organizational affairs. • The external environment acts in a somewhat unstable and unpredictable manner. • The external environment questions organizational expertise and challenges the power of school officials. • The external environment demands a piece of the action at virtually every point in the decision-making process.

Figure 4.1.   *Continued*

Adapted from Patterson, J., et al. (1986). *Productive School Systems for a Nonrational World.* Alexandria, Va.: Association for Supervision and Curriculum Development, pp. 40–41.

have power and who cannot. Decision making in rational organizations is a logical, problem-solving process leading to the one best solution for the organization. The environment external to the organization stays out of internal affairs, acknowledging the right of the organization to make its own decisions.

The nonrational view of organizational reality stands in stark contrast to the rational perspective. It states that organizations, in fact, are guided by multiple competing sets of goals most often arrived at through bargaining and compromise. The power to make things happen is distributed throughout the organization in very informal ways, and decision making is inevitably a bargaining process to arrive at solutions that satisfy a number of constituencies. Further, the external environment gets involved in internal affairs, demanding a piece of the action at virtually every point in the decision-making process. Although both the rational and nonrational frameworks offer plausible ways of thinking about organizations, the nonrational model more accurately describes the realities of organizational life within schools and school systems.

Reality #6 in Action

About four years ago, the superintendent in a progressive northwestern school district of three thousand students called the senior administrative team together to discuss future directions for technology implementation. The superintendent reminded the team that a representative committee had been formed six months earlier to set some district direction. That committee had attempted to rationally talk about the pros and cons of four major emphases: computer-assisted learning, computer-managed instruction, computer literacy, and administrative applications. Their discussion quickly turned into disagreements, with each school defending its own version of the status quo. After two more meetings with schools justifying their application as being most important, the committee had quietly dissolved.

The superintendent informed the administrative team it was time to move ahead on the issue. He posed the question, "What are our options?" The assistant superintendent said that, realistically, the options were limited. He commented that, "Even though we probably should engage in a systematic process to determine the highest priority application for computers, we're too far down the road to turn back. About 70 percent of our schools are emphasizing computer literacy while the rest that are using computers have concentrated on computer-assisted learning." In order to capitalize on the energy already expended, the assistant superintendent advised that schools be allowed to pursue either of the two goals. The team concurred, so the superintendent suggested that the original technology committee be reconvened to develop a rationale for the two goals and present recommendations to the school board within two weeks.

The process was set in motion. But once the superintendent's agenda for computers passed through the district's rumor mill, the school board was besieged by individuals and computer user groups lobbying for computer literacy to be the only goal of the district, at least for the present. When it came time for a vote, the board listened to two hours of community argument and voted four to three against the superintendent's recommendations. The board approved the single goal of computer literacy.

A week later, the local newspaper conducted a reader poll to assess the community's long-range expectations for computer technology. Seventy-three percent of the respondents answered "yes" to the question, Do you think the need for computer programming skills will be obsolete in five years? Eighty-two percent said "yes" to the question, Do you feel that using computers as a learning tool will be the most important computer skill five years from now? Succumbing to new political pressure, two weeks later the board reversed its original vote by a four to three margin in a surprise move by a board member who used the intricacies of parliamentary procedure to her political advantage.

Leadership Implications

The challenge for you and other leaders involved in organizational change is to provide rational leadership in the midst of a context that leans toward nonrationality. You can provide a measure of stability to the system by addressing each of the four categories in the rational/nonrational model: goals, power, decision making, and external environment.

School districts serve multiple constituencies, and sometimes the self-interest of these constituencies do not mesh. Such multiple and often competing organizational goals may leave the impression of aimlessness. But it is possible, for instance, to have separate organizational goals that attempt to meet the needs of different constituencies as long as these separate goals do not run contrary to the overall mission of the school district. One of your major responsibilities is to continuously clarify organizational goals in relation to the overall vision of the system. You must ensure that all proposed changes in district goals fit with the general direction in which the district is headed.

When people think of changes in power relationships, they worry that some people will gain while others lose. Given the nonrational perspective, you need to remind yourself and to assure others that empowerment can be an open-ended quantity. The power to make the most difference in the lives of children generally rests with those closest to the students. As an educational leader, you become more powerful by giving up control that you never really had in the first place and taking responsibility for providing others access to the support, information, and resources needed to make things happen.

Even as you empower others, never underestimate power as a motive in other people as they try to influence culture change or, more broadly, any other happenings in the organization. Sarason reflects on his long-standing research agenda regarding power in schools and comes to the following observations:

> I have to say that I underemphasized how power suffused *all* relationships in the culture: students vs. teachers, teachers vs. principals, principals vs. higher levels of administration, superintendent vs. board, board vs. political establishment, and the establishment vs. centers of power in the state capital. The problem of change is the problem of power, and the problem of power is how to wield it in ways that allow others to identify with, to gain a sense of ownership of, the process and goals of change. That is no easy task. It is a frustrating, patience-demanding, time-consuming process. (1996:334–35)

Sarason's advisory remarks underscore what other researchers have uncovered and what other practitioners have learned the hard way. It is another one of those "something we already know but don't want to talk about" items. As a leader of culture change, you need to accept the reality that power is a powerful motive in organizations. Your challenge is to work within the power, not be blindsided by it, as you lead the organization.

Despite the preference by some leaders to keep a tight grip on decisions in the organization, public institutions such as school districts are expected to open up the decision making to broad scrutiny and input. When this occurs, leaders know they run the risk of having to contend with the politics of bargaining, compromise, and concession. You can add common sense to the politics by creating decision-making processes that are clearly articulated, consistently followed, and aligned with core organizational values. One extremely helpful assistant to you in this arena is Kaner's *Facilitator's Guide to Participatory Decision-Making* (1996). This book is filled with conceptual frameworks and practical advice in how to facilitate groups in making group decisions.

Many leaders whisper to themselves, "If only external forces would just go away so we could do our jobs." From a nonrational perspective, you need to make the shift from if-only thinking to thinking that is more inclusive of the external environment. Because those outside the school district do have a stake in both the processes and outcomes of schooling, they deserve to be included in the school district's decision-making process. So you need to create expectations and procedures that allow this to happen.

You serve an equally important role by always scanning the external environment to anticipate what lies on the horizon. At times, you must deflect unwarranted criticism aimed at those working in the organization. At other times, you must accept full responsibility for attacks on the system by outside forces so those inside the system do not have to spend their energy on the politics of the situation. In both cases, you serve as a shock absorber so that external forces will not create significant disruptions to the work inside the system.

In your duty of scanning the environment, you also should stay on the lookout for external forces that are poised to invoke decisions on the organization. In fact, most school leaders point to externally imposed change as the greatest drain on organizational resilience. If you cannot deflect the externally imposed directives, you can at least apply the strategies discussed in this book to do damage control.

REALITY #7: MOST ORGANIZATIONS ARE WIRED TO PROTECT THE STATUS QUO

Some people like to describe organizations through the metaphor of a clock. If all the gears are functioning properly, the mechanism runs efficiently. Each gear interfaces with and depends on its neighbor to work properly. When any gear fails to perform, the whole mechanism comes to a standstill and repair is in order. Viewing organizations through the mechanical lens leads to the conclusion that every unit (school or department) needs every other unit to function most efficiently as a whole. When all units are performing well, as the saying goes, "things run like clockwork."

Although the mechanical model holds surface appeal, it does not aptly describe the life of organizations. Organizations are more appropriately characterized as organic. They are living, growing systems in which the various units contribute to the vitality in complex ways, not in simple, mechanical fashion. To review a theme I developed in chapter 2, this organic entity called organization has a pulse called organizational culture, composed of what the organization values, what the organization does, and what it says it values and does. These dynamics get summarized in slogans like "how we do business around here." Understanding organizations as organic cultures, not mechanical components, becomes critical in accepting the natural tendency for systems to preserve the status quo.

Organizations have plenty of reasons to defend their wiring in defense of the status quo. First of all, organizational cultures are relentlessly bombarded by stimuli from the external environment demanding culture change. To illustrate the point, I examined the offerings of products and services by one of the most respected national educational leadership organizations. What I found were the following categories of offerings. In parentheses is the number of offerings in each category:

- Assessment (104)
- Curriculum (104)
- Leadership (220)
- Learning (272)
- Standards (105)
- Teaching (448)
- Technology (38)

Knowing the caliber of this educational organization, I know also that the vast majority of these products and services are of the highest quality. So a single national organization has in its arsenal over one thousand bombshells ready to drop on your little organization at a moment's notice. Just to pick a few choices at random, are you interested in becoming a standards-based principal, assessing and improving the culture, building and enhancing staff morale, building shared responsibility for your schools, or addressing adult conflicts in the school community? No wonder school cultures feel overwhelmed by the choices to improve. And, unfortunately, the tendency of organizations toward resistance typically does not allow the system to differentiate between necessary and unnecessary change. O'Toole (1995) summarizes the power of the status quo by explaining that individuals are what they believe, and groups are their culture. Therefore, to require a group to change its shared beliefs is to threaten its very existence. From the perspective of an organizational culture, operating within the status quo certainly has stronger appeal than opening the culture up to the possibility of nonexistence.

Another reason that organizations defend their status quo tendency is that most cultures feel like they are pretty good the way they are. When outside forces try to bring positive changes into a culture, the organization sees the dilemma in terms of a trade-off. The organization can swap its current culture, built up over many years of accumulated wisdom and habits, for a promise by an outsider that things might be better in the future. As Farson describes this phenomenon, when confronted with culture change, organizations have to give up the pictures they have of themselves, pictures that have been developed over a lifetime: "These self-images or self-concepts are all they have to identify themselves. Understandably, to abandon them could be deeply threatening" (1996:102). Organizations have evolved their norms, shared values, and habits over a long period of time. No wonder the culture protects what it has proudly nurtured.

Reality #7 in Action

The school board of a fast-growing southwestern community is comprised of four senior managers in various businesses in the community and one parent activist. According to the school board minutes from a retreat, the board believes that customer service will be a major shift in thinking for schools in the future. Virtually every other type of organization has made the shift to being more responsive to customers' needs. Some organizations made the shift voluntarily, while others were forced into this position. The school board feels a strong obligation to seriously explore the concept. For starters, they want to look at school choice and charter schools. The school board directs the superintendent to convene a task force representing a cross section of perspectives in the community as well as a representative from each school in the district to examine the two concepts.

The superintendent has not expected this. She conveys her feelings to anyone who will listen. Principals and teachers get caught up in the emotion of this thing called customer service. They vehemently object to the idea of school districts viewing students and families as customers, and they strongly resent the idea that parents could pull their children out of their "home" attendance areas. In short, the immediate response in the district to the board's interest is overwhelmingly negative.

In turn, the board is surprised by the district staff's reaction. Board members argue that the very reason schools are in business is to serve the community's students and families. They decide to hold a series of forums in each school to discuss, logically and thoughtfully, the board's perspective and to listen carefully to others. Each forum is packed with people eager to be heard, and each unfolds in a similar manner. The teachers say they were hired to teach the students living in that attendance area and, furthermore, students are not customers and education is not a business. Teachers and administrators claim that a move to school choice and charter schools will allow parents to make decisions based on teacher popularity, babysitter convenience, and other noneducational factors. Parents at the forums argue just the opposite points. They claim that they have a right and responsibility to make decisions in the best interests of their children's education and that charter schools and school choice will be a step in the right direction.

After three months of heated debate, the teachers' union circulates a petition against the new ideas raised by the board. Ninety-three percent of the teachers sign it. When the petition is presented to the board, union officials argue that nobody can prove that student performance will increase under the proposed plan. They claim also that the school district is just fine the way it is. Students are learning, teachers are teaching, and most parents are satisfied with the quality of education. In their final plea, the union officials ask each board member to comment publicly on why he or she thinks the status quo is not good enough. Eventually, the board grudgingly withdraws its proposal because members believe the dissension is sapping too much energy from everyone to make the effort worthwhile.

Leadership Implications

The harsh reality that organizations are naturally wired to protect the status quo has major implications for leaders. First and foremost, leaders have to come to grips with the reality. If you are a leader trying to accomplish change, you are asking the organization to perform an unnatural act, an act that can drain organizational resilience. So be aware that the organization *naturally* will resist your efforts, however well intentioned.

Another, related implication of attempting culture change is the reality of the chances of success or, depending on your orientation, the chances of failure. Without mincing words, the odds of achieving culture change are incredibly slim. Barth echoes these sentiments when he confesses, "All school cultures are incredibly resistant to change, which makes school improvement—from within or from without—usually futile" (2002:7). Farson's view (1996) is that organizational cultures change more often as an invasion from the outside or rebellion from the inside. The assorted reasons for this reality, put forth throughout this book, fall into the category of things we already know but do not want to talk about. I feel compelled to restate, so there is no misunderstanding, what Sarason repeatedly warned school leaders to expect: the more things change, they more they stay the same—or get worse. I also feel compelled to restate that you should not use this reality as a reason or excuse to give up on helping the organization grow. Throughout this book you find plenty of strategies to overcome the odds of failure and to increase resilience.

A third implication of pushing the culture beyond the status quo is the assorted types of attacks on you as implementers of the culture change push back. Heifetz and Linsky reported:

> People respond to attempts at culture change in the following ways. You may be attacked directly in an attempt to shift the debate to your character and style and avoid discussion of your initiative; you may be marginalized, forced into the position of becoming so identified with one issue that your broad authority is undermined; you may be seduced by your supporters and, fearful of losing their approval and affection, fail to demand that they make the sacrifices needed for the initiative to succeed; you may be diverted from your goal by people overwhelming you with the day-to-day details of carrying it out, keeping you busy and preoccupied. (Heifetz and Linsky 2002a:65)

The researchers explain that people act this way because by attempting to undercut you, the culture as an organism strives to restore order, maintains what is familiar, and protects itself from the pains of culture change. The culture wants to be in equilibrium again, and you are in the way. If you anticipate that these attacks could indeed happen, you can develop contingency strategies for dealing with them, thereby positively affecting your resilience.

A fourth implication of this reality is what is required from you to lead change imposed by you. If the organization you are leading is heavily wired for protection and if the culture change you have in mind is absolutely crucial for organizational vitality, then you may need to resort to what Schein (1999a) calls "coercive persuasion." Below, I recap Schein's explanation of the source of the term and the reasons why he argues that this approach to culture change has merit.

"Coercive persuasion" as a concept was first used by Schein in his research on the seeming conversions and collaborative behavior of prisoners during the Korean War. A substantial number of civilians came away from their imprisonment being convinced of their "guilt." Schein elaborated:

> I described the process these prisoners went through as "coercive persuasion" to indicate that if a prisoner was physically restrained from leaving a situation in which learning was the only alternative, they would eventually learn from a process of "cognitive redefinition." They would eventually come to understand the point of view of the captor and reframe their own thinking so that the judgment of having been guilty became logical and acceptable. In effect, they had undergone what might be called a "conversion" experience except that it did not happen in the sudden way that religious conversions are often described. (1999a:165)

Linking coercive persuasion to culture change by leaders, Schein continues:

> When we speak of culture change, we are typically demanding levels of cognitive redefinition that can probably only be achieved by some version of coercive persuasion. To make stable changes at this level requires more than behavioral change. It requires the learner to reframe the situation, to learn new concepts and to develop new attitudes and ways of thinking and feeling or the behavioral changes will not last once the immediate incentives are removed. (1999a:166)

Your responsibility, therefore, in leading culture change is to help others reframe the situation to see it from the perspective of best-case outcomes; guide them in strengthening their skills and attitudes so they can feel "up to the task" demanded by the changes; and keep in mind the other harsh realities that are mitigating against your successfully leading the culture change initiative to fruition.

A final implication of this reality is the amount of time it takes to achieve culture change, if it is achieved at all. O'Toole (1995) points to the fact that for nearly five decades American industry was able to resist the ideas of such eminent thinkers as Peter Drucker and W. Edwards Deming. In educational organizations, researchers such as Fullan (1991); Kanter, Stein, and Jick (1992); and Sarason (1996) conclude that successful change takes from seven to ten years to implement before it truly becomes part of the organizational culture. Schein warns leaders, "It is likely going to be a long and difficult road, so one should not kid oneself that cultures can be ordered up and cooked like restaurant meals" (1999a:169). Sarason's warning is expressed in even more strident terms:

> We are used to hearing that in life we can count on only two things: death and taxes. We can also count on our resistance to change. If we can count on it, the fact is that school reformers only pay lip service to that fact, witness the unrealistic time perspective informing the efforts. Somewhere in their thinking they know the road ahead is rocky and they know why. But when I have examined as I have countless times, programs for change, several things become obvious. There is little or no thinking through, *in the planning process*, the extent, sources, and strength of predictable resistance. There is no serious effort to identify those personnel who will feel their ox is being gored. Little consideration is given as to the different ways those personnel can be given incentives to change. A time perspective or schedule is adapted that vastly underestimates the complexity of what is being attempted, as if the guiding assumption is that God is on their side, reason will curb or dilute the passions of resistance, and that there is a high correlation between what people say they do (or will do) and what they actually do (or will do). The usual result is that when the reformers begin to face the realities of the change process, their frustration, anger, and impatience mount; subsequently, either they employ what power they have (or seek to increase) in authoritarian ways, or they psychologically begin to disengage from their commitment to the effort. (1996:338–39)

So, given that the deck is stacked against culture change in the first place, trying to rush the change just increases the odds of failure. You increase the chances of successful culture change by realistically calculating how long it takes to get there.

Argyris does a good job of summarizing the assorted caveats about resistance to change:

> Anyone who has planned major change knows 1) how difficult it is to foresee accurately all the major problems involved; 2) the enormous amount of time needed to iron out the kinks and get people to accept the change; 3) the apparent lack of internal commitment on the part of many to help make the change work, manifested partly by people at all levels resisting taking the initiative to make modifications that they see are necessary so that the new plan can work. I reviewed my notes from 32 major reorganization initiatives in which I played some consulting and research role. I did not find one that could be labeled as fully completed and integrated three years after the change had been announced. That is, after three years there were still many people fighting, ignoring, questioning, resisting and/or blaming the organization without feeling a strong obligation personally to correct the situation. (1999:25)

With all of this gloom and doom about resistance to change, understandably you may conclude that it is simply not worth it. Before you rush to judgment, however, let me refocus on another central point that may have gotten lost in the gloom. Culture change is about leading the organization to a higher level, driven by your passion about the organization's need to change what it believes, does, and says. If the organization needs the culture change you propose in order to remain a vital culture, then here is what you need. Come to terms with the natural tendency for organizations to protect the status quo; confront the odds of success when attempting culture change; realize the painfully long time it takes for an organization to unlearn its old values, habits, and attitudes then relearn the new cultural values and actions; weigh what is at stake and what is at risk. Then in the final analysis, when the evidence accumulates that culture change is requisite to the vitality of the organization in the future, get about the business of making it happen.

REALITY #8: MOST ORGANIZATIONS INITIATE CHANGE WITH AN EVENT-DRIVEN MENTALITY RATHER THAN VALUE-DRIVEN MENTALITY

Most organizations move through their organizational life in an event-driven fashion, not anchored to a set of organizational principles that focus the organization's resilience capacity and direction. In this context, the term *event* does not refer primarily to the usual image of events, such as back-to-school night, the annual talent show, and the academic awards banquet. Related to organizational change, *event* driven means that change is characterized by a series of episodes, unconnected to each other, unconnected to a core set of principles, and occurring for a short time before being relegated to the proverbial last-year's-new-thing shelf.

Pick a topic: brain-based education, curriculum mapping, site-based management, data-driven decision making, standards-based assessment, multicultural education. Each of these topics has core educational principles as a foundation. Each has the potential of contributing to a value-based school district. But a breakdown occurs when school districts embrace these (or other) initiatives simply because it seems like the right thing to do at the time, whether it is the *right* thing politically, emotionally, financially, or educationally.

Organizations do not intend to be event driven. They sincerely believe their actions are based on core organizational values. In fact, most can even point to a laminated mission statement hanging somewhere. But, despite good intentions, organizations sap their resilience chasing a string of disconnected initiatives that end up on the junk heap of failed reform. No wonder it has become almost a mantra in teachers' lounges to say: This too shall pass. Been there, done that, got the T-shirt.

Reality #8 in Action

For nearly twelve years, the superintendent of a small school district in the upper Midwest managed to avoid what he considered the fad of school-based management (SBM). Things were running rather smoothly. The board left the operations of the school district to the superintendent and the superintendent left the teaching to the teachers. Operationally, however, the district functioned in a very traditional style.

All administrators reported to the superintendent, and he made most of the significant decisions, with occasional input from administrators who had demonstrated their loyalty over time. Then conditions changed. Two new board members were elected on a platform of opening up the system to more involvement. Parents started asking about their role in district decision making. Teachers began raising questions about who determined school budgets, who set the annual school calendar, and who participated in textbook selection.

To satisfy these pressures, the superintendent reluctantly sent a team of board members, administrators, teachers, and parents to a three-day conference on SBM. They returned as converts to this concept, armed with reams of documents on how to implement SBM. After a series of school board study sessions, the board directed the superintendent to develop a strategic plan on SBM, including the following elements: decentralized school governance, school improvement councils, and parent advisory councils. The plan was to be fully implemented in two years.

The superintendent complied with the request. But he was quick to send messages informally to the principals that they were the decision makers in the schools. He let the teachers know that they were the professional educators and parents were not. And he let everyone know that the final authority to make district decisions belonged in the superintendent's office. But despite these undercurrents, the district proceeded with setting up school improvement councils, parent advisory councils, and building-level leadership teams. Once established, all of these groups struggled with role, purpose, decision-making authority, and a lack of direction from the superintendent.

Over the next three years, both board members elected on the platform of opening up the system left the board for various reasons. The governing structures that had been established started to disintegrate when conflicts occurred and people did not know how to resolve them constructively. Teachers found themselves sitting on too many committees, which they believed diverted their attention from students. Principals did not like committees meeting all of the time without their involvement. And the superintendent clearly was uncomfortable with this encroachment on management rights.

Over the course of five years, school district operations slowly but steadily shifted back to the traditional model. When a newly elected board member asked what happened to SBM, the typical reply was that it was too much work, that people did not like being distracted from their main responsibilities, and that the traditional way of doing business was much more efficient: everybody knew their place.

Leadership Implications

If event-driven organizations are the norm, how do leaders do something as unnatural as creating value-driven organizations? As expected, the answer is, "not easily." In fact, in Glickman's (2002) study of Great American Schools, the schools typically devoted several years to developing an internal set of beliefs. But returning once again to the difference between optimism and hope, leaders who believe it is moral, right, and just for organizations to be value driven do whatever it takes to make it happen. Below I outline four steps to take as you lead toward becoming a value-driven organization: be clear about core values, understand the core values hierarchy, construct comprehensive core value statements of belief and action, and use core values to collect periodic feedback.

Leaders have an obligation to understand thoroughly the distinction between core values and other terms that are forecasts, observations, or descriptions of reality. In this context, core values are defined as statements of your organization's convictions. To put it in question form, "What does your organization care deeply about?" Your answer to this question becomes philosophical statements that give meaning and direction to your intentions, your actions, and the consequences of your actions. So you create school rules, form school improvement councils, and develop school–community councils. As a value-driven school leader, you do these things not because you want a bunch of new activities to monitor. You engage in these initiatives because of core values that drive your actions.

As you move to a value-driven organization, be clear about the three levels of values: ethics, core educational values, and topical educational values. Ethics are core values that express what your organization believes about right and wrong. Concepts like integrity, trust, and honesty are examples of values that sit at the top of the core values hierarchy, giving guidance to all you do in your organization. At the next level on the hierarchy are core educational values. These values center on what

matters most to you related to organizational focus. They signal how
your organizational energy should be spent when faced with competing
demands on your time. Examples of core educational values include the
following:

- We value creating a school environment that holds adults and students to the highest of expectations.
- We value creating a safe and nurturing environment where all students can learn.
- We value placing improved student learning at the center of all we do.

In our research on successful schools in the face of adversity (Patterson
et al. 2002), a major theme running through all of our interviews was
that there are no exceptions to the expectation that all students will succeed. And the schools that were most successful at this value matched
their actions with their words. The third level of core values focuses on
core values about specific educational initiatives. As I mentioned at the
beginning of this section, many school districts launch culture change
initiatives without investing the time to clarify, both to the leaders and
the entire organization, *why* the organization is launching a new initiative. In the school-based management (SBM) scenario above, school
leaders felt compelled to respond to the push toward site-based management, without investing the reflective time to figure out what they
valued underneath the slogan of SBM. In contrast to the scenario where
districts moved toward then away from SBM, successful change initiatives anchored their actions in values such as:

- We value involving people in decisions that affect their professional lives.
- We value diversity of opinions.
- We value creating conditions so all voices can be listened to with respect and dignity.

In situations where schools invest their collective energy in a common
set of core values rather than wasting individuals' energy chasing slogans,
the culture change initiative has a much greater probability of success,
and the school has a much greater chance of maintaining resilience.

Even if you have taken the important step of creating core organizational values, you are not finished yet. There is a second step to help complete the "core value package." Specifically, you need to construct a set of *we will* statements that describe concretely what the organization will do to make the core value become operational in the organization. For example, suppose your school district develops the following core value: "We value creating a climate of caring and support throughout our school." Once the core value is constructed, staff still do not have a clear determination of what is expected of them on Monday to make the core value come alive. So you take the companion step of developing as a school staff a set of *we will* statements that give added meaning and clarity to the value. In other words, the core value package, as illustrated below, gives both those inside and outside the organization a clear picture of what you care about and what you will do about it:

Value: We value creating a climate of caring and support throughout our school. Therefore, we will:

Provide a safe environment for teaching and learning to occur
Provide professional support through materials, time, and instructional guidance
Show concern for the well-being of all who work and learn in our school

If your school takes the steps I have outlined so far, you have made great strides to focus on what matters most to your school. However, there is another crucial step to take to help ensure that the core value packages become part of the culture of your organization.

What if your organization developed core value packages around these values: communication, excellence, respect, and integrity. People would be impressed with your statement of values. However, just for the record, these are the same core organizational values that appeared in the Enron organization's 2000 Annual Report (Lencioni 2002). So just displaying a set of values is not sufficient to make your organization value driven. To complete the cycle of moving core values into the overall culture of the school, I recommend you consider the following three-step process.

First, collect data on importance and implementation effectiveness. It is not enough to develop a bunch of statements about what you value and what you will do. School leaders need to deliberately and systematically collect information about "how's it going?" As a concrete example, let's use the core value package above, converting it into a "Feedback Inventory." As shown in figure 4.2, you can ask two key questions for each statement in the package: "To what extent is this statement still important to us?" "To what extent are we effectively implementing the statement in our daily practice?" By using an instrument similar to the Feedback Inventory in figure 4.2, you can concisely display the data you collect about importance and effectiveness in order to give you information about how to move ahead.

A second step is to conduct a gap analysis to identify areas for follow-up action. Drawing on the data you collect in step one, you have a snapshot showing the areas with the greatest gap in scores between importance and effectiveness. Let's suppose your Feedback Inventory shows an importance score of "5" for the item: *Show concern for all who work and learn in our school.* Suppose, also, that your effectiveness score for that item is a "2." With a gap score of "3" between importance and effectiveness, your school flags that area as an area of focus to bring better alignment between what you say is important and how well you are implementing the area of concern.

Step three, use gap analysis information as a basis for constructing an action plan, is the straightforward process of developing a task/timeline framework, like the one outlined in figure 4.3, so you and your staff know what is expected in order to strengthen your school culture relative to creating a climate of caring and support.

Key Point	Importance	Effectiveness	Gap
We value creating a climate of caring and support.			
We will provide a safe environment for teaching and learning to occur.			
We will provide professional support through materials, time, and instructional guidance.			
We will show concern for the well-being of all who work and learn in our school.			

Figure 4.2. Feedback Inventory

Topic	School Climate of Caring and Support
Goal	Show concern for the well-being of all who work and learn in our school

Task	Timeline	Leadership responsibility	Resources needed	Indicators of accomplishment

Figure 4.3. Action Plan

In working with schools and other organizations for many years in the area of core values, I am the first to acknowledge that the challenges in carrying out the steps are painful and arduous. In fact, when presented with the requirements necessary for shifting from event-driven to value-driven organizations, many leaders find themselves saying, "We can't afford to invest the time and energy to do this right now. With so many things piled on our plates, we cannot be spending precious time talking about values." The harsh reality is that leaders cannot afford *not* to. The vitality, even the survival, of the organization is at stake.

REALITY #9: MOST ORGANIZATIONS ENGAGE IN LONG-TERM CHANGE WITH SHORT-TERM LEADERSHIP

Today, most people have moved grudgingly to the point of acknowledging that organizational change is inevitable. Many people even say that they can live with it, but they are quick to offer the following conditions: Make sure whatever needs to be done is done all at once; do not have it be too disruptive; do not let it cost very much; and, by the way, do not let it affect me.

Deep inside, we all know that these conditions cannot be honored. Something we already know but do not want to talk about is that there are no shortcuts. As I discussed at length in Reality #7, culture change often takes more than ten years to plan, implement, and institutionalize before it becomes embedded into the culture of "how we do business around here." This means an organization needs to persistently and passionately pursue a single initiative for more than a decade in order to increase the chances that the change will stick. Add to the mix the reality of multiple initiatives occurring simultaneously, and the conclusion is inevitable. Long-term changes call for long-term leadership.

The harsh reality, however, is that school systems function with short-term leadership. Over 50 percent of the nation's superintendents serve in positions for less than six years (Cooper, Fusarelli, and Carella 2000). In urban districts, where the need for long-term change is more acute, turnover among superintendents is even more frequent. For example, the Council of Great City Schools reported that forty-two of forty-seven urban districts had hired new superintendents since 1990 (Yee and Cuban 1996). Leadership in higher education presents a similar picture. In a study by Ross, Green, and Henderson (1993), 53 percent of college and university presidents served for less than five years. Even though these statistics can fluctuate and be analyzed in different ways, one conclusion stands out. On the average, organizational leaders leave before organizational initiatives have a chance to succeed.

Reality #9 in Action

A small city school district on the East Coast benefited from the leadership of a talented female superintendent for seventeen years. When she retired, the board appointed the assistant superintendent to the superintendent's position without advertising the position. The new superintendent was constantly compared to the previous one and came up short on most measures. During his tenure, he tried to switch the administrative salary schedule to a performance-based system. He also mandated a new clinical supervision model for teachers and a rotating system for moving principals around every three years. Additionally, he installed the concept of consensus bargaining. In twelve months he was quietly encouraged to leave.

The next time around the board conducted a national search and hired a person from the West Coast. The new superintendent arrived with impressive credentials and a strong track record as a tough decision maker. After six months in office, he scrapped consensus bargaining because he believed that the negotiations process was not about reaching consensus; it was about taking tough stands in the best financial interests of the taxpayers. He favored a different teacher supervision model and proceeded to personally train all administrators in the process. Finally, he started an adopt-a-school project with the business community. This model had been a big hit in his previous district. Unfortunately, after a year on the job he had to retire due to illness.

The board appointed an interim superintendent who had recently retired after forty-one years in a neighboring district. He served until the beginning of the next fiscal year. During his tenure, the board put all recent initiatives on hold.

After another superintendent search, the board voted four to three to hire a particular candidate. When the local newspaper published the board's split vote, the candidate withdrew her candidacy The second choice candidate had already accepted a position in another district. The board did not want to start another search so close to the beginning of the school year, so they promoted the high school principal to the superintendent's position for a one-year term, with the understanding that he could apply for the position when it was posted again.

The high school principal did apply and was elected in a five to two vote by the board. As superintendent, he aggressively pursued new initiatives in the areas of block scheduling, inclusion, and portfolio assessment. And he returned the administrative compensation system to a salary schedule like that used for teachers because administrators did not like being compared with each other. Three years later, due to board turnover, the superintendent found that the board no longer supported him or his initiatives.

With the revolving-door syndrome for superintendents in this district, the editorial page writer for the local newspaper raised a very logical question, "What initiatives have survived the upheaval in leadership over the past seven years?" People were hard pressed for an answer.

Leadership Implications

What can be done to break the pattern of attempting long-term change with short-term leadership? Given that there is no shortcut to long-term change, the search for solutions shifts to the area of leadership. The most direct solution is somehow to increase the length of tenure for people in leadership roles. Although easier said than done, if school boards and superintendents are truly committed to making culture change work, then school boards need to find ways to make a corresponding commitment to the executive leadership. Currently, superintendents find themselves in a predicament similar to coaches. When the track record of success starts to become blurred by a few losses, the coach is fired. The owners remain. The system remains. When school districts chalk up a few losses in the eyes of the community, symptomatic relief comes in the form of a new superintendent. Virtually every other member of the system remains in place. A longer-term commitment between board and superintendent would increase the chances for seeing culture changes bear fruit.

If the turnover rate cannot be altered substantially, school systems are left to seek consistency in district direction from multiple superintendents. According to Fullan and Watson (1991), what it will take is a leading superintendent with a tenure of five to seven years, followed by another successful superintendent for a similar term deliberately selected to complement and extend the district's work. Fullan and Watson caution that, under the best of circumstances, it is going to take two or three successive superintendents all working from the same fundamental commitments to organizational change to institute effective change. The success of this approach depends on a collection of school board members understanding and accepting the need to secure long-term leadership direction.

Having core organizational values drive the system is vital to achieving long-term district direction with one or multiple superintendents. If school districts anchor themselves to core values, these values can transcend the tenure of superintendents and governing boards. In fact, the core values become the basis for selecting future leaders, both at the board and administrative levels. The stability of the organization then rests on the extent to which the values shaping the future transcend the personalities and power of those providing leadership at any given point in time. In two landmark studies of visionary companies that have stood the test of time, the researchers found that the distinguishing factor separating truly outstanding organizations from their closest rivals was the concept of organizational values. The great companies, those built to last, maintained their stability across economic cycles and changes in executive leadership because of their long-term commitment to the values that drove the system (Collins and Porras 1994; O'Reilly and Pfeffer 2000). School districts have the capacity to provide similar stability. All it requires are people in leadership roles who truly care about the long-term vitality of the organization and who demonstrate their caring by implementing policies to secure "longer term" leadership. The primary burden for this responsibility falls heavily on the shoulders of school board members and superintendents.

REALITY #10: MOST ORGANIZATIONS EXPECT THE GREATEST AMOUNT OF CHANGE WITH THE LEAST AMOUNT OF CONFLICT

Just living and working in organizations today pushes people to their limits. Then, on top of the energy demanded to do daily work, organizations expect employees to expend additional energy adapting to overlapping, nonstop change, all of which occur under the organizational banner of good intentions. Organizational leaders know that if they do not act like they are moving ahead, they appear to be falling behind. They feel pressed to show demonstrable evidence that the organization is systematically engaged in meaningful change. In short, the proverbial organizational plate is piled high. Many would argue *too high*. So when the organization extracts time, effort, and energy from employees engaged in change, leaders know they cannot afford to have additional energy spent dealing with conflict related to the change. Organizational change initiators typically think, "let's just act like adults, get the job done, and set aside personal agendas. We don't have extra time to waste on conflictual issues." Many leaders even worry that acknowledging the conflict might send signals to everyone watching that things are not under control. If things are not going smoothly, then someone will need to be held accountable for straightening them out. That someone usually is the leader.

In many respects, individuals within the organization also want conflict to just go away because they are acutely aware of the chain reaction. Conflict creates tension. Tension forces people to confront the reality that harmony is missing. Absence of harmony signals that something is wrong. Whatever is wrong will need to be fixed. And trying to fix conflictual situations or relationships is not easy. So to put an abrupt halt to the potential chain reaction, people pretend that conflict does not exist.

Leaders and other employees can mask the conflict temporarily. They can push it away from direct exposure. They can even shoot the messengers who speak of conflict. But they cannot ignore it away. In the long run, suppressed or even denied conflict will erupt into dysfunctional behavior, organizationally and interpersonally, and it will cost everyone.

Reality #10 in Action

For several years, a middle-class school district in the Southwest carefully studied the concept of including special education students in "regular" classrooms. A committee reviewed the pertinent literature, made site visits to districts recommended as cutting edge in this area, and involved people from multiple perspectives in deliberations. The committee recommended implementing the inclusion concept throughout the school district over a three-year period. The board was proud of the work by the committee and accepted its recommendation. The superintendent was proud of the professional way the committee discussed the complex issues and came to a consensus decision. And the teacher groups were proud of the way people rallied around the core beliefs of inclusion.

Then came the time for implementation. With very good intentions, "regular" education teachers welcomed students with disabilities into their classrooms, along with their teachers. The special education school was closed and students with severe needs returned to their home attendance areas.

After a while, though, the reality of this fundamental shift became more apparent, and tensions started to mount. Special education teachers no longer had their own classrooms. Regular education teachers were no longer alone in their classrooms, and they began to realize they did not have the necessary training or skills to adapt the curriculum and assist the special needs students. Students began complaining about the disruptive behavior of the integrated students. Parents complained about the lack of attention their own children were receiving. School principals found themselves caught in the middle because they could see the viewpoints of the various groups.

The superintendent was soon criticized because conflict was not the accepted norm in the school district, and the school board wanted to know what the superintendent was going to do to quell the disturbances. The superintendent called a special meeting and admonished people for not acting professionally He reminded everyone in the room that they had approved the inclusion plan and that the entire community was watching them. In closing the meeting, he said, "It's time for everyone to get along, act professionally, and keep your complaints to yourselves. Our students are depending on you to implement this plan with a collegial spirit. Any questions?" With no questions forthcoming, the meeting ended and people filed out of the room silently, taking their conflicts with them.

Leadership Implications

So what can you as an educational leader do to alter the natural tendency to avoid conflict? First, personally accept the reality that conflict is inevitable. It is endemic to all relationships, organizations, civilizations, and species. Conflict is not the issue. Conflict is the condition. The issue centers on how you choose to handle the conflict. Leaders need to move beyond phony harmony by acknowledging that conflict in organizations is natural and all right. In other words, phony harmony exists when you reinforce the expectation that everyone in the organization should carry on about "how wonderful things are, how everyone functions as one big happy family, and how no problems can be found in our house." On the other hand, when you set the tone that conflict is expected, that it comes with the territory of people working together, then you can treat the condition of conflict in a nonjudgmental way and move toward addressing the real issue: how to get through the conflict to a satisfactory resolution.

A second thing you can do is to create a safe environment for confronting conflict in a constructive way. By valuing the energy of dissent, you can show people inside and outside the organization that honest conflict in a safe environment provides the seeds for rich solutions to organizational issues. When conflict surfaces, move to the tension point, not away from it. The tension can be used creatively by capitalizing on the energy of dissent and leading people to reach solutions everyone can accept.

Third, support the training necessary for all organization members to become more skilled in conflict resolution and consensus building. Conflict brings out the deepest differences in perspectives and amplifies the diversity among group members. Therefore, groups must have the requisite skills to use conflict as positive energy in pursuit of a strong collective decision. One school district, for example, trained every employee in conflict resolution skills. It even took an additional step by training approximately twenty employees, from all job classification areas, to be facilitators for other groups in the district. When an elementary school staff had difficulty resolving an issue about who supervises recess duty in cold weather, the school requested that a pair of facilitators attend a staff meeting to help them work through their differences. This strategy for resolving conflict is one way of sending a message throughout the organization that conflict is normal. The key is to resolve it in a constructive way.

REALITY #11: MOST PEOPLE AND ORGANIZATIONS DENY THAT THE OTHER TEN REALITIES ARE, IN FACT, THEIR OWN REALITY

While working on the previous sections of this book, I had a troubling feeling about writing this section regarding denial. I knew it was not going to be easy or fun to elaborate on the reality about people and organizations denying their own reality. Then, the evening before I wrote this section, reasons for my uneasiness began to unfold. It all began as dinner conversation with my wife. I said, somewhat tentatively, that I was not looking forward to writing the section on denial. But I did not know why. I proceeded to think aloud about how I would approach the topic. Maybe I could do a pretest and posttest to see if readers changed their perspectives about acceptance of the harsh realities after having read this much of the book. Maybe I could challenge readers to accept the realities if they want to be effective in the future. Or perhaps I could ask readers to identify situations in their own professional experiences when, upon reflection, they now realize they denied these realities.

As I said these words, I could not help feeling as if I were being too rational and logical about this. It is not rational. It is emotional and painful to confront one's own denial. Suddenly, a little voice inside my head said, "To prove the point, Mr. Author, why don't you write about your own experience with denial of some of these realities?"

Well, now what? I turned to my wife and said, "You know what I need to do? As painful as it is going to be, I need to confront my own experience with denial. I don't like even to entertain the possibility that I ever acted first in my own self-interest, acted as a victim, or refused to understand the *what* and *why* of messages people were sending me. But to better understand the magnitude of what I'm asking other leaders to confront, I need to feel, first-hand, what it's like." Reluctantly, therefore, I will describe a real-life situation in which I personally suffered because of some of the harsh realities discussed in this book.

In 1988, I was selected to serve as superintendent of the fastest growing school district in Wisconsin. The district justifiably enjoys a fine reputation for the quality of education, and the district, as well as the entire community, possesses a fierce sense of pride in its reputation.

But we can all stretch and grow. The board asked me to provide leadership in making some changes that would better position the district for the future. So I did. During the first four years of my tenure, we moved heavily and swiftly into SBM. Other companion initiatives included consensus bargaining, Issues Resolution Councils, revision of the teacher evaluation model to a more collegial approach, movement toward inclusion in special education, mandatory intensive training for all new teachers in state-of-the-art teaching, conversion of all-administrator meetings to leadership development sessions for graduate credit, reorganization of central office staffing, and conflict resolution training for all district employees. And I am sure my former colleagues could add many more items to the list.

As these initiatives accumulated, the system started to send out messages of circuit overload. People asked me to slow things down. Board members said they were getting the impression that it was too much, too fast. Employees throughout the district complained that they did not have enough time to do any of these initiatives adequately. So what did I do? When I first began to feel and hear the mumblings about my moving too fast, I rationalized that *they* were not moving fast enough. When the messages got louder and more widespread, I got louder about the importance of all the good things that were underway. I found myself selling the virtues of the many new initiatives as what was in the long-term best interest of the organization. The more I pushed, the more loudly people said, "we are initiating a lot of important stuff, Jerry, but we're not implementing very much of it very well."

Someone said that we live life forward and understand it backward. As I lived through the flurry of initiatives that I encouraged as superintendent, it all made such good sense. I thought I was acting in the best interest of the organization. I thought I was listening to what employees were telling me. I thought I was the architect and they were playing victim.

Several years later, I now see things differently. Now that I am compelled to reflect on this time period (understand it backward), I realize that I was denying my own reality. I was putting my own self-interest first, not the interests of the organization. It is not that I was being selfish. It is just that my own interest as leader was to position the school district for the future in as many ways as possible, as fast as possible. In other words, *I* decided it would be good for people. The people who were trying very hard to carry out the initiatives were also trying to tell me that it was in the organization's long-term best interest to slow down so energy could be spent on quality implementation.

As people were saying these things, upon reflection I suppose I did not want to know the *what* and *why* of the message they were sending. I denied that their view was, indeed, real. If I accepted what they were telling me, then I would have to assume responsibility for making some adjustments in my own vision for the district and in my own pace for leading the district. As long as *I* did not get the message, *they* would continue, from my biased perspective, to be responsible for not moving fast enough.

A third reality I lived was the role of victim. When the talented employees throughout the district started resisting the volume and pace of new initiatives, I took on the silent martyr role. I said to myself, "Look at all the neat things we're trying to do. Look at how visionary you've been, Jerry. Look at how much better positioned the district will be five years from now if we are able to pull off these initiatives. And what do you get for all this? People want to return to the good old days. I deserve to feel sorry for myself." So I assumed the victim role. And I am sure I acted out some of the other harsh realities also.

I now realize that, as a result of my denial of these realities, several initiatives quietly disappeared because the system did not have enough energy to spend on fully implementing them. Of course, I had good intentions. But as someone else said, "Isn't it ironic that we want to be judged by our intentions, and we judge others by their actions or the impact of their actions." I deeply feel that my intentions were honorable. My actions, however, caused people a lot of stress.

I close this section by acknowledging that *all of us* have the tendency to deny the harsh realities, including me. And I can say now that it would have been in the long-term best interest of everyone in the district, including myself, for me to have resisted the denial path and to have chosen the path of acknowledging what I needed to do to alter my own reality.

REALITY #12: MOST PEOPLE AND ORGANIZATIONS *DO* HAVE THE CAPACITY TO DEVELOP RESILIENCE IN THE FACE OF THE OTHER ELEVEN REALITIES

Clearly, it is not easy for people and organizations to alter their tendencies toward the first eleven realities. But individuals and organizations do have the *capacity*—the ability plus the will to make something happen—to increase their resilience. The following is a review of the major points leaders need to remember when working to effect real, lasting culture change.

- Invest ample time in understanding the various group members' self-interests and find ways of meeting those interests while, at the same time, doing what is best for the organization.
- Help members of your organization see connections between particular change initiatives and the general direction in which the organization is headed. Also, build into the system specific procedures that require people to assume responsibility for personally understanding proposed change initiatives.
- Create a sense of urgency for major change by selling the change initiative on the principle of pain. Expose the reality that the pain of not changing will be greater, in the long run, than the short-term pain of changing.

- Strengthen interpersonal trust by engaging in authentic, intentionally redundant communication about the proposed change. Show how this change connects to the core organizational values. And be open to examining your own conduct and acknowledging times when your behavior did not measure up to your own publicly professed values.
- Strengthen organizational trust by building into the system procedures that allow people to challenge, without fear of retribution, the conduct and intentions of those initiating change.
- Help individuals see that they do, indeed, have a choice between being victims or architects of change. Help others move from operating out of their worst fears to operating from a belief in achieving their highest hopes. Then provide the support, information, and resources needed to help people be architects rather than victims.
- Acknowledge that school systems tend to be nonrational and apply four basic strategies for leading in a nonrational environment: (1) continually clarify the organization's goals in relation to the organization's overall vision, (2) empower people by believing in them and letting go of traditional notions of controlling leadership, (3) create and consistently follow clearly articulated decision-making processes aligned with organizational values, (4) serve as a shock absorber so external forces will not cause major disruptions to those working within your organization.
- Help people see the urgency of supporting the proposed change. Appeal to people's emotional side by demonstrating that each individual's future well-being is at risk if change is not achieved.
- Create reflective time within the organization's routine operations to achieve a common understanding and commitment to core values. Develop strategies within the system to hold people accountable for aligning practices with these values.
- Develop a long-term commitment to long-term organizational direction. Build stability into the system by establishing core values that transcend the personality and power of any individual leader.
- Accept the reality that organizational conflict is inevitable and create a safe environment for constructively handling conflict. Support conflict resolution and consensus-building training for all members of the organization.

- Resist the natural tendency to deny the harsh realities of organizational change. Instead, acknowledge them and apply strategies to help your organization become more resilient in adapting to change.

Up to this point in the book, I have offered guidelines to help leaders build resilience into organizations by acknowledging some harsh realities about organizational change and then developing leadership strategies to move ahead in the face of adversity. In chapters 5 and 6, I focus on the next major piece of the puzzle for leaders: helping others and themselves develop individual resilience.

5

STRENGTHENING RESILIENCE
IN OTHERS

Anyone can lead under normal conditions. The true measure of an effective leader is the one who helps the organization stretch to a higher level despite adversity. As I have worked with organizations for more than thirty years, rarely have I encountered an organization that says, "We have no problems here. Everything is under control. We have no significant barriers that produce adversity and anxiety in this organization." To the contrary, virtually every organization I have been fortunate to work with literally has filled pages of chart paper with adversities negatively affecting their ability to achieve the central mission of improved student learning. At the same time, our research on resilient organizations (Patterson et al. 2002) uncovered schools that, despite adverse conditions, have documented track records of successful academic achievement within a caring, supportive environment. This chapter summarizes three leadership strategies that have proven effective in helping those in the organization become more resilient.

MAINTAIN HIGH EXPECTATIONS FOR STUDENTS AND ADULTS

Two little words summarize one major contributor to resilient school cultures: No excuses! This theme was conspicuous in schools throughout our travels across the United States. As one school leader succinctly put it, "There are absolutely no excuses for failing to produce achieving students. None. Zero. Zilch. I mean *no excuses!*" Although a lot of schools talk about no excuses, the truly resilient schools convert the talk into action by creating school cultures driven by the following beliefs:

- A schoolwide belief that all students can succeed.
- High expectations for students in the face of adversity.
- Instructional practices that are aligned with beliefs about school success.
- Frequent assessment of student performance relative to benchmarks and follow-up with appropriate actions.
- Reward and recognition systems that honor success in achieving high expectations.

Resilient schools took the slogan "all children can learn" and moved it to the action level by constructing core value packages similar to what I described in Reality #8. In one school, for example, the principal and teachers invested considerable time crafting this core value package:

Value: We value placing a central focus on student success for *all* students. Therefore, we will:

Constantly convey that staying the same is not good enough

Implement strategies for charting student progress to staff, the student, and parents of the student

Incorporate diverse teaching strategies that are responsive to the diverse learning styles among our children

Mobilize virtually all of our school's human resources around the theme of success for *all* students

Set budget priorities based on our commitment to student success

Avoid instructional fads and other distractions that take us away from our central focus

The core value package became a basis for the school staff conveying in no uncertain terms what they stood for regarding the question of who can succeed. In other words, the schoolwide belief that all students can succeed was crafted to clearly say what people inside and outside the school culture could expect from the organization. In turn, staff resilience was strengthened because people were part of the craftsmanship. They owned the core value statements. They knew what the school stood for, so they knew how to spend their energy points to achieve greater resilience.

During so-called normal times, it is rather easy to be true to the mantra of high expectations. When the going gets tough, though, the natural tendency is to lower expectations. Suppose, for example, that your school is part of a community that has experienced a slow but steady shift in student demographics. Ten years ago, people regarded your district as one of the elite suburbs attracting upwardly mobile families. However, for the past decade the impact of a large chicken processing factory in your community has resulted in a student population that currently is 54 percent Hispanic. The socioeconomic level of the community has dramatically changed, partly due to the infusion of a migrant labor force and partly due to an exodus of the upwardly mobile families looking for less diversity. The result, of course, is a student composition with much greater academic needs. The natural tendency is for a school staff to lower expectations for students. The school becomes a victim of the adversity. In contrast, resilient schools that we identified operate from a schoolwide belief that adversity will not undermine high expectations. As one school leader told us, "We are committed to figuring out how we can make it through the adversity without lowering the bar of high expectations."

Resilient schools have learned, over time, that staying the course of improved student learning means staying attuned to the level of alignment between "What we truly believe" and "What we actually do." As I discussed in chapter 2, healthy organizational cultures pay attention to the alignment among the culture anchor-points of Believe, Do, and Say. In the case of resilient schools, the leaders and the staff pay close attention to make sure that their professional energy is spent on instructional practices that produce successful students, in spite of whatever adversity appears on the scene.

In our research, school leaders and classroom teachers told us repeatedly that student progress needs to be constantly monitored against high expectations that have been set by staff. The monitoring is not intended to be a "gotcha" approach. The purpose of frequent assessment is to stay on top of student learning so that adjustments can be made instructionally on a timely basis. As one principal told us, "We know where the kids are in October (relative to end-of-year expectations). As painful as it is to be assessing in the fall the students' possibility of making the assessment targets in the spring, it is less painful than getting to the end of the year and the students not meeting the benchmarks." As an outgrowth of this assessment, the teachers knew that it is part of the school culture to change their instructional practices for certain students. These changes were resilience building, not resilience draining, because the school culture reinforced the belief that teachers are not expected to immediately have all of the answers about how every student can be successful. To the contrary, teachers are told that it is OK, even encouraged, to experience temporary setbacks on the road to school improvement.

Another finding from our research was that resilient school leaders did not let imposed assessment demands by outside forces derail them from their mission. Resilient school leaders came to terms with the reality that the state department of education, for instance, had every right to expect students to demonstrate proficiency in literacy skills. And even though the schools may not have selected the state assessment model as their top choice for getting there, they accepted the state-imposed model as reality and devoted their energy to making it work on behalf of their passion for student success.

Schools that function effectively even though they have plenty of reasons not to find plenty of ways to celebrate success along the way. At the classroom level, teachers understand the power of small wins. A fourth-grade teacher told us, "I say to the child, 'look at the progress you have made; if you keep doing that, at the end of the year this is where you are going to be.' Because the child has to have some hope, too. Small wins. Also it gives me a target to shoot for, because I know that I can pull the child up."

At the school level, school leaders constantly search for ways to reward and recognize staff members who make contributions to student learning under rough conditions. Strategies include sending notes to the parents of the *teachers*, telling the spouses of teachers how much the school leaders realize the personal sacrifices being made on behalf of the students, and spending significant time in classrooms as a show of support. Through all of these actions, the prevailing message is consistent: resilient schools gain strength by honoring success of students and success of staff.

CREATE A CLIMATE OF CARING AND SUPPORT

In our search for resilient schools, we found that high expectations alone were not sufficient for building resilience. In fact, some schools enforced high expectations through a culture of fear and intimidation. Students and adults complied with tough standards because they knew the consequences awaiting them if they failed to measure up. Their resilience accounts, however, were nearly depleted. The truly resilient schools achieved high expectations within a school culture known for caring and support for the students and adults who reside there. Our research documented that resilient leaders led the way in a schoolwide commitment to caring and support by concerted attention to creating a safe environment for teaching and learning to occur, showing caring and personal support to others, and providing time, money, and other resources to support the mission of the school. In this section, I highlight some of the strategies used to sustain the resilience strength of caring and support.

The resilient schools we visited did not waste energy bemoaning the conditions of their school's community. The people we talked to treated the poverty, mobility, and violence within the community as just another harsh reality. They were steadfast, though, in their belief that they did have an influence over the sense of community within the school. Specifically, school leaders acknowledged that sometimes you have to start with the value of tough love in order to set the stage for learning to occur. As one urban middle school principal summarized his challenge upon entering the job: "The first three to four years, I concentrated on getting the overage students out of the building. I had to be hard and tough to let the kids know I cared. And caring means giving them a safe place to learn." In resilient schools, both staff and students felt safe to go about their work.

Under any conditions, all of us need to feel a sense of caring by others. The need becomes especially crucial in a setting characterized by adversity. When resources are scarce and students walk through the schoolhouse doors each day with adversity stamped all over them, the precious gift of personal caring goes a long way in strengthening resilience. For an adult, personal caring can take the form of colleagues and school leaders taking the time to know about family members, reaching out in times of crisis, and knowing about the personal interests of the adult. For a student, personal caring shows up in actions such as making the student feel welcome in the school and letting parents know about the successes of the student. Although all of these examples seem so straightforward, we have learned that adversity seems to get in the way of people maintaining their focus on caring. In resilience-building schools, this sentence sums up the school culture message: "You are important, you can do it, and we will not give up on you."

When adversity hits, many times it takes the form of diminished resources. Nonresilient school leaders typically fall into the victim trap. They take the posture, "If only we didn't have scarce resources, we could do a better job around here." In stark contrast, resilient school leaders facing the same adversity respond with, "Given the harsh reality of scarce resources, how can we find the time, money, and other resources to achieve our mission of student success?" Just by framing the question as "and" thinking instead of "if-only" thinking, school leaders help create added resilience capacity. Here are some of the ways we found in our research that resilient schools make it happen. Principals in resilient schools realize that the gift of time is one of the most precious resources that can be provided. So they go into classrooms as instructors in order for the teacher to have a bit more reflective time; teacher leaders manage their schedules so they can provide relief when a teacher needs to be out of the building to take a sick child to the doctor. Other teachers volunteer to take a person's class for the day so the person can attend a professional workshop. All of these efforts become more deeply appreciated because they happen despite the fact that adversity offers plenty of excuses for people to selfishly guard time as their own private commodity.

Another precious commodity made more valuable by adversity is money. As I write this, more than forty states face budget shortfalls this fiscal year. Education particularly is being hard hit. With no money forthcoming, school leaders face the apparently impossible task of creating more money from less. Not to be deterred, resilient leaders work with their staff and their community to increase the pace of grant writing, reorder budget priorities to make sure the money is spent on the central purpose of student learning, and turn to the community businesses for financial help. Realizing that these efforts will not turn poorly funded schools into rich schools, school leaders know that the mere fact that everyone is pulling together to make the most out of the financial adversity is a strength in itself, independent of the dollar amount on the other end of all of the efforts by the school culture.

In schools facing ongoing adversity, nonresilient school leaders typically respond by placing materials under lock and key. Teachers have to beg for a ream of paper or access to the copy machine. Other school leaders, those who consciously take steps to strengthen resilience, realize that access to materials becomes a rich resource. In one of these schools we visited, a teacher summarized her school's view of access: "I hear people talking who teach at other schools and the supplies are all locked up. The supply warden guards them. That just doesn't happen here. We have an open supply closet, and we go in and get what we want. It makes us feel like professionals." In another school, the teachers reported that having access to the keys to the school was an inexpensive, symbolic act to send the message that teachers are valued as professionals and trusted to come into the building at any time to do their work. In all of the resilient schools we had the good fortune to visit, resilience was manifest in the fact that the school refuses to be a victim of circumstances. They choose, instead, to take action to help shape their own future.

HELP PEOPLE MOVE FROM ENDINGS AND TWEENER TIME TO NEW HORIZONS

The resilience-building leadership strategy of helping people move through endings and loss, Tweener Time, and new horizons draws on the extensive work of William Bridges (1991). What he found was that, once a decision had been made to implement an organizational change, leaders generally had definite plans about how to accomplish the logistics of the change. They set in motion strategic plans, action plans, or other similar labels that capture the who, when, and how of organizational change. But typically missing from these plans, Bridges discovered, was the human dimension. So he developed a framework to help leaders find answers to these questions: How do leaders support individuals through the ambiguity of leaving the familiar and not yet arriving at the future? How do leaders help people find their places in the changed organization?

One resilience-building strategy that leaders use is to help others in the organization make the distinction between external changes and internal transitions. For example, most people can identify with the experience of trying to fly from one city to another, only to encounter a few problems along the way. Nagging disruptions to even the most carefully made plans can include delayed flights, missed connections, and waiting in line for lost luggage. These unexpected events represent changes that happen to people. But the events that happen are only one piece of the change process. Another piece is how people individually adapt to the changes. Some people who experience these airline problems lose their tempers and lash out at the airline staff. Others bury themselves in a good book to make the time pass more quickly. In other words, the way people internally cope with external changes reflects their resilience when confronted by adversity.

At the school and district level, leaders can take specific steps to help people make the internal transitions through external changes in the most healthy way possible. The first hurdle to clear is to help people deal effectively with endings and loss. Every culture change, for instance, causes loss. Even positive changes individuals embrace require people to give up things. As a school leader, you cannot assume that planned, positive culture change comes without a price for individuals. Instead, you must identify the types of losses that will be incurred and devise strategies for helping people deal with them constructively.

Suppose, for example, that the school board has targeted the movement of sixth-grade students in your school to go to the newly opened middle school. As principal, you need to anticipate the types of losses the school faculty will experience. For one thing, they will lose connections they once held, including relationships, memories of the past, and perhaps parts of their personal identity. As a resilience-building strategy, you can help them find ways to honor the loss of connections by designing strategies that allow them to celebrate the past, talk about the connections being given up, and put to rest fond memories. One way of achieving this is to participate in activities symbolizing "burying of the past," allowing individuals to grieve the loss of their connections. All too often, leaders want the pain to go away for others, so they try to hide the fact that loss is occurring. For instance, some leaders believe the cold, hard facts should be enough to convince people that moving sixth graders to the middle school demands a celebration, not a wake. Instead, you need to encourage the unfolding of the grief process as natural and necessary.

Another major loss most individuals experience during organizational change is the loss of territory. Territory can be as concrete as the special wing of a school or as intangible as the loss of perceived stature. Not surprisingly, physical trappings and sphere of influence serve as markers of individual power or status in organizations. You can assist those losing territory by acknowledging the loss as real and important to the individual, and by helping individuals move beyond the view that territory dictates status. In the example of students moving to the middle school, you can help the sixth-grade teachers by arranging a special meeting between them and the middle school principal for a special viewing of their new classroom space. And you can support the teachers' request that they get to retain some of the furniture and equipment they have acquired over time.

A third type of loss is the loss of meaning. If people do not understand the *why* of organizational change, then the change becomes nonsense, and individuals believe they are being forced into meaningless change and out of a world that had a lot of meaning for them. You, therefore, need to be a meaning maker. In a practical sense, you need to point the way by showing the sixth-grade teachers how the change will enhance their self-respect and well-being. You can emphasize, for instance, that the sixth-grade teachers will be the experts on the developmental needs of this age level and that the more content-oriented seventh- and eighth-grade teachers will be turning to them for guidance.

Finally, loss of control represents a tremendous barrier to overcome as individuals struggle with the prospect of change. The feeling of powerlessness is debilitating. Most vulnerable are those whose self-esteem or confidence is tied to being in control of the details of their lives. To break through the barriers, you need to work hard to provide individuals with options. Given the reality of change, how can the individuals affected have some say in the outcomes of what happens? Returning some semblance of control through choice can help return order and stability to the lives of those affected by change. In other words, you can assist the sixth-grade teachers who do not want to make the leap to middle school by paving the way for them to put in transfer requests for elementary teaching jobs in other elementary schools in the district.

In summary, you can strengthen the resilience of those suffering loss by paying close attention to the powerful impact that personal loss has on people's ability to adapt during the change process. Correspondingly, you can build into the system strategies and structures for helping individuals successfully adapt to the changes at hand. Resolving the loss in a productive manner results in a smaller drain on individuals' resource accounts as they encounter the second phase of transition.

"Tweener Time" is the confusing period when the old reality has been jettisoned and the future has yet to be determined. Marked by instability, ambiguity, and a feeling of being leaderless, this time calls for measures that produce temporary stability. In your school leadership role, you need to put into effect interim rules, policies, organizational structures, and whatever else it takes to help individuals make sense of the organization's apparent drifting. During Tweener Time, for example, some organizations have implemented a formal transition team charged with monitoring the progress of the change. This team plays an important role as a clearinghouse for rumors, new information, and creative ideas. You need to anticipate old baggage from the past surfacing again, and you need to expect that dissident voices will get louder. The transition team is one mechanism for keeping you informed about these forces (Bridges 1991). In the example above of transferring students and teachers to the middle school, a transition team composed of teachers and students from both the sixth grade and seventh grade could meet on a regular basis to address issues and fears, as well as plan transition activities, such as the sixth graders coming to the middle school a day or two before the opening of school to learn the school layout and where their classrooms will be located.

Individuals emerge from Tweener Time as the changes in the organization begin to take shape in front of their eyes. What seemed like an eternity with the organization adrift at sea now seems to have form and substance. As long as employees see hope for themselves, they can also see hope for the rebirth of the organization. Individuals need help at this stage establishing their place in the "new" organization. The middle school principal, in the scenario above, needs to be out in front, developing orientation programs to increase the sense of efficacy for sixth-grade teachers in their new assignment. The principal also needs to provide individual and group support as people adapt to their new professional world.

As you sharpen your resilience-building strategies to lead people through culture change, you will find (as you already have in your experience) that individuals have varying needs to ease the pain of change. However, I also have found that there are four things that everyone needs from the organization in general, and from you as leader in particular. Regardless of their level of support for the change and irrespective of their place in the power structure, everyone needs caring, clarity, choice, and hope.

People need to believe that the leaders of the organization care about them. This does not mean that the organization should operate in a caretaking mode, allowing people to view themselves as victims of major organizational change. But people want to work in an organization that shows compassion, empathy, and concern for the individual.

People also want clarity. They want the security of knowing how the organization works, where it is heading, and what they might experience along the way. They constantly seek out any bits of information that will remove ambiguity and limit the depletion of their resilience accounts as they strive to understand their places in the organization.

People need to feel they have choices. Whether the choice is as complex as designing new job descriptions or as basic as a choice to stay in the school or not, choice provides people with some sense of control over their future. In fact, Froiland's (1993) research study of twenty-one variables found a sense of personal power, one's choice over the use of time, resources, and workload, to be the only predictor of who stayed healthy in work situations. People without this sense of choice over their professional lives were unable to cope with high amounts of pressure and change.

Finally, people desperately need hope. They need to believe that tomorrow, whether defined as the next day or the next few years, will bring energy, renewal, and harmony to their lives in the organization. They want to be believers in the organization, and they want the leaders to give them reason to be hopeful.

From your perspective as a leader, the challenge of providing caring, clarity, choice, and hope might seem overwhelming. The needs of the employees are genuine, and there are no foolproof leadership checklists. However, there are some guidelines that might be helpful to you. In figure 5.1, I list a series of questions (adapted from Bridges 1991) for you to consider as you respond to the call for caring, clarity, choice, and hope.

	Endings and Loss	Tweener Time	New Horizons
Caring	• How have we acknowledged the losses with empathy? • How have we permitted people to grieve and how have leaders publicly expressed their own feelings of loss? • How have we found ways to help people compensate for their losses?	• How have we found ways to help people feel that they still belong to the organization? • How have we demonstrated that people are still valued in the changing organization? • How have we provided support, information, and resources to help people move ahead? • How have we modeled authentic listening and empathy for people's concerns and worst fears?	• How have we found new ways to reward people for making it through the Tweener Time and becoming energized again? • How have we found ways to celebrate the new beginnings? • How have we created strategies to allow people to confront their feelings about losses when the emotions reoccur?
Clarity	• How have we given people accurate information, redundantly, in multiple ways? • How have we clearly defined what is over and what is not? • How have we made it clear that the endings are necessary to put the organization in a more productive position in the future?	• How have we created temporary policies and procedures to get through the Tweener Time? • How have we structured communication and decision-making channels to keep open dialogue flowing during this uncertain period? • How have we created temporary roles and reporting relationships amid uncertainty?	• How have we continued to clarify the purpose of the change and where we are in the journey? • How have we modified and clarified our communication and decision-making channels in the new organization? • How have we revised and communicated the policies, procedures, and priorities consistent with our new beginnings?

Figure 5.1. Caring, Clarity, Choice, and Hope: Questions for Consideration by Leaders

Continued

Choice	• How have we developed a plan to give a choice to take part of the past with them into the future? • How have we given people a realistic choice not to participate in our future and, at the same time, helped them to create other choices in the new work environment?	• How have we encouraged people to experiment and to take risks to create their own futures? • How have shifted from thinking about losses to thinking about how people can discover new ways of doing things?	• How have we ensured that people have a voice in the roles they play in the new organization? • How have we provided support for people to choose another work environment if they are not satisfied with their place in the new organization?
Hope	• How have we given people sufficient reasons to see that letting go of the past will be worth the effort in the long run? • How have we helped people come to terms with the reality that all new beginnings must involve endings?	• How have we conveyed our dreams for a new beginning? • How have we developed concrete plans so people can see the hope being approached systematically? • How have we provided special training programs so people have the skills to be successful in the new organization?	• How have we helped people see that the long-term gain was worth the short-term pain? • How have we involved people in the crafting of a long-term vision? • How have we positioned ourselves for a strong organizational culture?

Figure 5.1. *Continued*

The questions are organized according to the three phases of transitions I described earlier, namely, Endings and Loss, Tweener Time, and New Horizons.

As you initiate or otherwise assume a leadership responsibility for culture change, make sure you do not get so caught up in the issues involved in implementing change that that you fail to attend sufficiently to the human dimension. Stay focused on the *people needs* of the organization by helping those affected by culture change move from where they see themselves in relation to the change initiative to where they need to be in order to become more resilient.

6

INCREASING YOUR OWN RESILIENCE

Even when you do all of the "right" things helping others successfully move through culture change, you still pay a personal price. In this chapter, I first address the reality of the pain of leadership; then I present concrete strategies to help you reduce the pain and increase your resilience.

THE ANATOMY OF LEADERSHIP PAIN

The head pain usually comes first. These are the pains related to thinking through what is in the best interests of the organization as you contemplate major organizational changes. This is not only an extremely painful period, it is a time when the loneliness of leadership gets even lonelier. The long hours spent, on and off the job, privately agonizing over the merits of initiating significant culture change start to take their toll.

Those of you who have initiated change before and experienced the pain have a pretty keen sense of the organizational price paid. You know there is no escaping it, so you invest heavily in the head pain of thinking about the potential change from every conceivable angle. Is this the right thing to do? Do we have the organizational energy to pull it off? Am I the right leader for what needs to be done? Once you have struggled intellectually with these issues and concluded that significant change is in the best interests of the organization, the pain in the head gets overtaken by another kind of pain—back pain.

Back pain refers to the anguish you feel when others blindside you. Back pain may have the highest hurt index among the various pains of leadership. One reason for the extraordinary hurt of back pain can be traced to the element of surprise. Generally, you do not see it coming, and you do not always know who is causing it. Also, in contrast to other pains of leadership, back pain is external. It is one thing to bring pain on yourself. It is quite another to have others do it to you. The back pain becomes particularly acute when it is inflicted by those you trust the most. Betrayal is the lowest form of back pain, and the sting lasts a long time. As a leader, your best form of resilience when faced with back pain is to remain authentic in what you say and do. Stay true to your ethical convictions (your core values) and your commitment to your organization. You likely will be tempted at times to show you can play dirty too, but the high road will always be your best choice. When tempted to play dirty, remember this: "Never wrestle with a pig. You both get dirty and the pig loves it!"

No other pain of leadership lasts as long as the pain to the heart. It hurts deeply to bring pain into the lives of others as you ask individuals to abandon what they have known and done for so many years. Leaving the security of old values and moving to the uncertainty of a fundamentally new way of doing business inevitably carries great pain. So why would you deliberately be hurtful to others and bring heart pain to yourself?

The short answer is that you do not have a choice. Your pain comes from knowing that what you do will be painful to others. You know also that if you do not move others to a different way of thinking and acting, the pain will not be any less. In fact, it will be greater for everyone. So you lead others through the rather immediate pain of letting go of the old ways, suffering loss in the process, and ending up in a more rewarding place. Or you manage people who dodge the current pain, only later to encounter the delayed pain of holding on too long to the past. Even your own heart pain grows more excruciating if you fail to influence those in your organization to accept current, short-term pain to achieve potential long-term gain in the future.

Leaders readily admit that the pains of leadership are not confined to the head, the back, and the heart. There is the pain in the neck from all of the annoying obstacles, the pain around the eyes from wearing blinders too long, and the pain in the foot from shooting yourself over stupid little mistakes. These pains of leadership became much more personal when I conducted research on the life of superintendents, which culminated in a book, *The Anguish of Leadership* (Patterson 2000). I interviewed fourteen people who have spent their professional lives preparing for and then serving as school superintendents and who have distinguished themselves in this important role. My intent was to simply tell the story of the superintendency through the eyes of the men and women who lived the experience. What I got was something else.

As I listened to the superintendents reminisce individually about the time spent in the top slot, I was struck by the commonality of their stories, which could be summed up by the old Clint Eastwood movie title, *The Good, the Bad, and the Ugly.* Each superintendent talked about the good times—times when they tackled tough problems with the support of the board and community. But for most, the erosion of board support—the bad—led to frustrations great and small that piled up along the way. One superintendent described this period as putting rocks in your pocket:

> My advice is simple: Watch out for rocks in your pocket. If you're doing your job right, eventually you will start accumulating rocks in your pocket from alienating certain groups or individuals because you can't please all of the people all of the time. As you gather the rocks, no single rock may seem at the time particularly heavy . . . although I've been known to collect a few boulders right on the spot. Anyway, as you collect the rocks in your pocket, the cumulative weight will start to take you under. (Patterson 2000:32)

The veteran superintendent had just been fired by his board. He had no significant retirement income. He understood about having rocks in your pocket.

While each superintendent I interviewed painted a picture that included significant accomplishments and personal pride, each picture included some moving snapshots of the ugly toll the superintendency takes on the soul. One toll is the personal toll the job takes on the superintendents themselves. But, as I listened to their words and observed their tears, I realized what was really difficult—the truly ugly—is the toll this job takes on their families. Antonio Guerra became animated when the conversation shifted to his family. He leaned forward in his chair, locked his eyes onto mine, and confessed:

> They really do hurt your family. Our home life is open (for public inspection) where any glimpse of our personal life is used against me. They've hurt my son and daughter as students in the school district. They've hurt my wife as someone who has a tough job being a superintendent's spouse. My wife has had to endure tremendous hardships, even worrying about who she can be friends with. And when she does become friends with someone, they use that for their own personal vendettas. These are high prices you pay and it's a high-stakes game. (Patterson 2000:50)

I came away from these interviews with the distinct impression that the pain inflicted on family during the superintendents' professional struggles created more personal anguish for these men and women than the pain aimed directly at them. I sensed also that a measure of relief was afforded them during the interviews as they could finally candidly discuss their rage at the injustices their families silently suffered because of their career choice.

Even if you do not fill the superintendent's shoes, the leadership role you occupy has its own anatomy of pain. As with the superintendents I interviewed, some measure of relief for you can be found in bringing the discussion of the anguish of leadership out in the open to talk about in a healthy away. But merely talking is not sufficient. You need to develop and hone a set of resilience strengths that will help you personally move ahead in the face of adversity. As an outgrowth of my work that produced *The Anguish of Leadership,* I decided to conduct research aimed at identifying leadership resilience strengths. In the next section, I draw upon this research to summarize what you can do to stay resilient during the tough times. For each resilience strength I describe, I list a set of reflective questions for you to consider.

RESILIENCE STRENGTH: STAY FOCUSED ON CORE VALUES

In chapter 4, I outlined a set of strategies to help schools stay focused on core values. Specifically, I presented a format that schools, or any other organization, can use to articulate what they stand for (We Value statements) and what they will do (Therefore We Will statements) to make the values come alive in practice. The same model applies to you as an educational leader. You gain resilience when you invest the time up front to become clear about what you value and how you will act consonant with your value. For example, in the domain of ethical values, what do you value about being trustworthy? What will you do on a daily basis to demonstrate your trustworthiness? Below is a sample of what a school leader's core value package on trust might look like:

Value: I value acting in a trustworthy way at all times. Therefore, I will:

Do what I say I will do when I say I will do it

Create forums for open communication about the extent to which I "walk my talk"

Regularly ask others to evaluate my conduct regarding alignment between my value and my practices in the area of trustworthiness

In addition to constructing core value packages and collecting feedback, you have other very important responsibilities that will help you stay focused on core values. First, resist the temptation to chase new initiatives. One school principal I interviewed in the resilience research said she was not going to chase anything until she saw if it had legs: "'When someone comes to a principal's meeting with a suggestion or a new idea, I make certain it has legs. Too many times we as educational leaders spend unnecessary resilience points worrying about some crazy new idea, when it may never sprout legs and take off running in the first place'" (Patterson et al. 2002:26).

A second strategy to increase resilience is to model what you stand for. Without exception, the resilient principals I met in the research process are role models for others. One principal modeled her core values about the importance of quality teachers by spending almost two hours on the interview process for new teachers. She explained, "'I invest this much time because I am going to have to live with that person, and this is a student's life that is at stake here'" (Patterson et al. 2002:28). Modeling also takes the form of letting people see the passion for what you do. Representative of the passion expressed by resilient leaders were these words by a teacher leader: "'My resilience is strengthened because I love what I am doing. Children are my passion, without question! I have a strong belief that we can make a strong difference in the life of a child'" (p. 28). Summarizing the sentiment of letting people see your passion, one leader put it succinctly: "'My job is to do whatever it takes, I mean literally whatever, to help the students and teachers be successful'" (p. 28).

Leading imposed school change presents a special challenge to your resilience as you simultaneously try to be true to your core values and try to implement change being imposed by outside forces. As I work with school leaders on this challenge, I am struck by how many leaders feel trapped into "either/or" thinking. "Either we have to implement the state mandates or we ignore state mandates, at great risk to us." This approach inevitably takes a toll on your resilience account.

I am also struck by this irony: one person's initiative is another person's imposition. When invited to talk with me about school change, school leaders and teachers do not talk about the changes that they have initiated. Instead they talk about those imposed changes that drain their resilience and detract from a focus on their own initiatives. According to school leaders, "Outside forces are at work trying to take us out of our game plan." This tension point between "us and them" is a perfect example of judging others on the basis of intentions, actions, or consequences. Invariably, people in the state department who impose state mandates are not mean-spirited people. Their intentions are honorable. Their actions, however, mandate culture change at the district or school level, often without the resources to support the mandates. One consequence is that you as a school leader resent the outside intrusion by those who do not appear to know or care about the culture of the school. Another consequence is that your resilience account starts to hemorrhage as you scramble to comply with ridiculous mandates you do not support.

To strengthen your resilience and the resilience of those you serve, I offer three guidelines when faced with leading imposed change (Patterson and Patterson 2001). First, avoid Reality #10. Do not deny the presence and power of the harsh realities. Examine each of the harsh realities, determine how each plays out in your organizational setting, and implement leadership strategies that position your school for long-term resilience. Second, make sure you are clear both on your own core values about the central theme of the imposed school change and the core values the imposers hold about the topic. As corny as it may seem, you need to know "where they are coming from." You need to know what they care about that causes them to believe the imposed culture change is worth doing. And if you are not clear on your own core values, then you put yourself in the awkward situation of complaining about what "they" are doing to you, without being clear about what you value that is different from their values. The third guideline reinforces what has been discussed in a previous chapter. Move from "either/or" thinking to "and" thinking. Faced with imposed school change, you may find yourself chafing at having to choose between what the central office or the state department wants and what your school wants. Being forced to choose between A and B creates a win-lose situation. A more resilient approach is for you to create a win-win situation by reframing the issue to create "and" thinking. You might ask, for example, "How can we be true to our own values at the school level and, at the same time, implement the imposed directive?"

To summarize the special challenge of maintaining your resilience in the face of leading imposed change, do not forget that the imposers of the change have good intentions. Do not forget that your change initiatives sometimes are considered impositions by those responsible for carrying out your initiative. Do not forget what you have learned in this book about leading despite adversity.

To help you consider in-depth how you demonstrate the resilience strength of staying focused on core values, reflect on the following questions:

- How, specifically, have I focused on being a value-driven, not event-driven leader?
- What have I done to determine, among competing values, what matters most to me?
- To what extent have I constructed core value packages, including values and *I will* statements, for my core values?
- How have I resisted the temptation to chase new initiatives?
- In what ways have I regularly modeled for others what I stand for?
- How have I applied resilience skills and strategies in leading imposed change?

RESILIENCE STRENGTH:
ACT ON THE COURAGE OF YOUR CONVICTIONS

Acting on the courage of your convictions under normal conditions does not negatively affect your resilience account. When things turn from good to bad or ugly, your resilience has a tendency to drop. This is when you need to draw on the strength of your core values and stand tall as you stare at the proverbial firing squad. Below I propose some benchmarks to help you gauge when you need to take action in defense of your convictions.

Under what conditions will the issue not go away? It is only human to hope that an issue will eventually just go away and leave you alone. Several of the superintendents I interviewed reported that they tried that strategy and it backfired. They ended up spending a lot of their resilience points trying to put out the fire as it raged out of control. Asking the question, *Under what conditions* will the issue not disappear? causes you to confront the *possibility* that the issue will hang around. If the probability is low that the issue will leave you alone, then it is time for you act to on the courage of your convictions.

What are the worst-case outcomes of ignoring the issue and the best-case outcomes of acting on the issue? By posing the questions in this way, you are compelled to consider the issue in a favorable light. If the issue can literally produce results that violate your convictions, you have an ethical obligation to act. By confronting what the worst-case outcomes might be, you force yourself to consider the impact of not taking charge. By asking the best-case question, you are obliged to consider the positive things that can come out of your actions. If you are willing to take the necessary steps to make the best-case outcomes happen, you send a powerful message to those you are leading. You are willing to take significant risks to make good things happen that are consistent with your core values.

What are the risks of failing? For any significant issue that has a possible impact on your own resilience, you should assess the odds of failing and examine what is at stake if you do fail. Particularly in leadership roles, repeated failure is not generally considered part of a true leader's track record. Also, by being clear on what you are placing at risk of losing if you fail, you can more clearly assess if the risk is worth it. As part of the risk equation, you also need to factor in the personal resilience risk of failing to act on your convictions, even in high stakes situations. If the values embodied in the issue are bedrock values that are important to you as a school leader, then I submit you need to be true to your values, irrespective of the odds of failing, or more optimistically, the odds of success. If you do not act on the values that matter most to you, then you end up succumbing to the pressure of being event driven, not value driven. And you correspondingly put a drain on your resilience. Conversely, even in the eye of the storm, being true to your convictions is a huge boost to your long-term resilience.

In summary, the resilience strength of acting on the courage of your convictions includes the risk of pausing to find the time and the safe environment to personally reflect on these questions:

- In what circumstances have I recognized when action was needed in order to be true to my convictions?
- To what extent have I checked to see if what matters most to me is in jeopardy?
- In what ways have I assessed the conditions under which an issue would go away?
- How have I assessed worst-case and best-case outcomes of acting on an issue?
- To what extent have I assessed the risks involving in acting on the courage of my convictions?
- In what ways have I viewed mistakes as another form of learning?

RESILIENCE STRENGTH: BE POSITIVE IN SPITE OF ADVERSITY

When you entered your first leadership assignment, you probably felt charged up and ready to save the world. Your resilience tank was overflowing. You were the epitome of a wild-eyed optimist. But along the way, something happened. More pointedly, some things happened. Each thing, each adversity, held the potential to put a dent in your resilience tank and convert you from optimist to pessimist. To help you avoid this temptation to become a convert to the dark side of leadership, I outline below some strategies that I learned from resilient leaders on how to remain positive in the face of adversity.

As someone once told me, you do not drain your resilience when you are surprised. You drain your resilience when you are surprised you are surprised. To keep this from happening, expect the world to be filled with disruptions! Disruptions to your expectations about how things should happen will happen. So, even though you may long for predictably stable conditions in your leadership role, the only predictability you can count on is the predictability of disruption. If, therefore, you expect the world to be filled with disruptions, you are not surprised you are surprised when disruption pops up. This orientation helps you make sense of the nonrational world and its accompanying predictable surprises and, furthermore, helps you preserve your resilience to move beyond the disruption. The positive spin on this is for you to take the disruption at hand and frame the question, "Given the harsh reality of disruptions to my best-laid plans, how can I move ahead?" You do not fritter away resilience points agonizing over the surprise. You simply put the disruption in perspective and maintain momentum toward a positive outcome.

A companion resilience-building strategy is to anticipate these disruptions whenever possible. Or, as one resilient principal offered her counsel, "I have three bits of advice: Anticipate, Anticipate, Anticipate." She went on to say that she anticipates worst-case outcomes, comes to terms with how she will move ahead if the worst-case outcomes do indeed happen, and celebrates when they do not happen. In other words, to strengthen your resilience build contingency plans for possible disruptions and hope that you do not need them. Resilient leaders will tell you that this is not wasted energy. You have been vigilant about what could happen and you have the resilience capacity to deal with the disruption. In his book, *Leadership,* former New York City Mayor Rudolph Giuliani talked about his approach to disruptions and anticipation:

> After September 11, I was frequently asked about staying calm in the face of crisis. As I have already discussed, it comes down to preparation. Throughout my time as mayor, we conducted tabletop exercises designed to rehearse our response to a wide variety of contingencies. We'd blueprint what each person in each agency would do if the city faced, say, a chemical attack or a biomedical attack. We went through how we'd act in the event of a plane crash or a terrorist attack on a political gathering. We didn't just choreograph our response on paper, either, but did trial runs in the streets, to test how long the plan took in practice. We even simulated an airplane crash in Queens and a sarin gas attack in Manhattan, eerily in the shadow of the twin towers.
>
> The more planning we did, the more we could be ready for surprises. Before September 11, there were those who said we were being overly

concerned. We didn't hear that afterward. Relentless preparation means not just preparing for disasters but anticipating potential trouble. (2002:62–64)

Giuliani concluded his thoughts on this topic of anticipation by saying that the lesson he learned was to prepare for anything he could think of so that he would be prepared for the thing he had not thought of. This example drives home the point that a combination of anticipatory outlook and contingency planning goes a long way toward maintaining resilience.

A third way that resilient leaders remain positive is to see opportunities where other people see obstacles. To illustrate the point, I share the story of two brothers.

One brother is a very sad and unhappy little boy who cried continually and just didn't know how to be happy. The other little boy was always happy, no matter what happened to him. The boys' parents were concerned about the extremes in the behavior of the children and decided to consult a psychologist. The psychologist prepared two rooms for the boys. The sad child was placed in a room filled with his favorite toys, cake, ice cream, and everything the psychologist believed would delight a child. The parents and psychologist observed the child through a two-way mirror as he hung his head and sobbed uncontrollably. The second child, the happy one, was placed in a room piled high with manure. They watched as the child dug happily through the pile. When they asked the child why he was so happy digging the manure, he replied, "With all this (manure), I just KNOW there's a pony in here somewhere!" (Patterson et al. 2002:118–19)

In a similar way, you have the option of interpreting what is happening to you as a leader in a positive way. Similar to what I described earlier in the book about making imposed change work for you, not against you, you build resilience by seeing opportunities in the midst of obstacles. I am not talking about denying that the obstacles exist. I am referring to the strategy of describing as accurately as possible the reality of the issue threatening your resilience, then using your energy positively to move ahead by acting on the opportunities contained within the reality of the issue. This approach is similar to how the Chinese reportedly think about crisis. According to Conner (1992:232), the Chinese express the concept of crisis with two separate symbols. The top character represents potential danger, while the lower character conveys hidden opportunity. Resilient leaders work within the crisis to make the opportunity dimension the dominant force of action.

One thing I learned from my research on resilient schools is summarized by a poster hanging in an assistant principal's office: "It's not so much what you do, it's how you think about what you do that makes all the difference." Instead of framing your challenges with a mindset of "I can't do that because of all the adversity I face," try reframing the challenge by asking, "How can I find ways to move ahead in the face of all of the adversity I face?" When you paint the circumstance with the broad brush of *how can I*, you open up options instead of shutting them down. The simple shift in language from "I can't" to "How can I" symbolizes a profound shift in thinking that will help you stay more positive and, in turn, more resilient.

A final bit of advice about remaining positive despite adversity: Do whatever it takes to find humor in the midst of adversity. Not only does it help you feel better to laugh in the middle of problems, it helps others. In my research I saw many examples where distress was relieved when the leaders were able to laugh about their problems. One teacher in a middle school described the impact of humor as used by her principal: "'The principal has an incredibly strong sense of humor and a very stress-free type of management. He makes us laugh just about every day. That leads to a positive environment in a place where you have a lot of stress'" (Patterson et al. 2002:123). You need to be able to laugh both at the absurdity of what someone or some "body" has imposed on you, and you need to be able to laugh at yourself. Finding humor in the ridiculous helps you put in perspective that it beats the alternative of whining or crying about the ridiculous. By laughing at yourself you are able to acknowledge your humanity, your vulnerability to mistakes, and then you can move ahead.

Without resorting to strutting around in rose-colored glasses, you can develop resilience strategies to help you remain positive despite plenty of reasons to become a pessimist. To guide you in how you are doing in this regard, I encourage you to consider the following questions for self-reflection:

- How have I handled disruptions to my expectations?
- To what extent have I anticipated disruptions and built contingency plans for them?

- To what extent have I engaged in "how can I" thinking rather than "I can't, because . . ."?
- To what extent have I found humor in the midst of adversity?

YOUR OWN NEEDS FOR CARING, CLARITY, CHOICE, AND HOPE

Just like I described in a previous section about how you can provide caring, clarity, choice, and hope for those you serve, you need it too. You need to confront and act on the harsh reality that you need the same things that everyone else in the organization needs. In figure 6.1, I present a series of reflective questions for you to quietly, seriously consider in the areas of caring, clarity, choice, and hope.

To illustrate how you can positively address your needs in these areas, find people who care about you as a human being and do not really care what kind of power and authority position you occupy. You also need to

Caring	Clarity
• How have I confronted signs of mourning in myself, and do I view them as natural? • How have I given myself permission to take a temporary time-out from decisions and responsibilities that can wait? • How have I carved out quiet times and stable places to give myself respite from the chaos I so often feel around me and within me?	• What exactly is going to be different for me because of recent changes? • What am I losing in the organizational changes? • Am I clear about why I feel such a heavy burden on behalf of the organization, even though I believe the changes I have made were the "right" things to do?

Choice	Hope
• How am I pushing myself to break out of old ways of seeing my life and the options available to me? • Have I set short-range objectives for myself to restore a sense of efficacy? • Am I prepared to confront the statement, "Career, you've been good for me and good to me. Now I'm ready to try something different"?	• How am I creating a new place for myself in light of the changes occurring in my life? • Am I allowing myself to play with outrageous changes in my professional path, viewing them as real possibilities in the long run? • Have I designed professional development opportunities for myself, so that I can stretch and grow into a "hopeful future"?

Figure 6.1. Personal Caring, Clarity, Choice, and Hope

do whatever it takes to take care of yourself. Heifetz and Linsky recommend that you find ways to stabilize yourself by "establishing a safe har-
bor where you can reflect on the previous day's journey, repair the psy-
chological damage you've incurred, renew your stores of emotional
resources, and recalibrate your compass" (2002a:71). Then they add,
"Whatever sanctuary you use, you need to use and protect it" (p. 71).

As a leader, you strengthen your resilience when you find ways to help
put things in perspective and bring clarity out of chaos. Heifetz and Linsky found in their research that leaders added to their resilience by identifying a confidant, "someone you can talk to about what's on your mind
without fear of being judged or betrayed. Don't confuse confidant with
ally. A confidant doesn't necessarily support the issue; he or she supports
you" (2002a:71). The confidant gives you a safe place to help make sense
out of what is happening around you and what is happening to you.

A third thing you need for your resilience is a sense of choice. Just like
I mentioned in the section about providing clarity for others, you need
to feel like you have professional options in your life, rather than feel
like you are trapped with no outlet for your anguish. Probably one of the
most resilience-draining traps for school leaders is to feel stuck in a job
with no escape. In recent research, Ibarra (2002) found that conventional, reasonable-sounding career change methods lead to the most dis-
astrous of results. Instead, she presented research-based recommendations to help you exercise choice over career options. "Most of us know
what we are trying to escape: the lockstep of a narrowly defined career,
inauthentic or unstimulating work, numbing corporate politics, a lack of
time for life outside of work. Finding an alternative that truly fits, like
finding one's mission in life, cannot be accomplished overnight. It takes
time, perseverance, and hard work. But effort isn't enough; a sound
method and the skill to put it into practice are also required" (p. 47).
The researcher offered a set of strategies to create real choices for you.

Above all else, you need a sense of hope. I want to bring us back full
circle to a point I made in the opening section of this book. There is a
distinction between optimism and hope. Optimism is the belief that
things will turn out as you would like. Hope is the belief in yourself that
causes you to fight for what is right, just, and reasonable, irrespective of
the consequences. Havel elaborates on this point when he says that, in
his view, hope is a state of mind, not a state of the world: "Either we

have hope within us or we don't. Hope is not a prognostication—it's an orientation of the spirit. Each of us must find real, fundamental hope within himself. You can't delegate that to anyone else . . . life is too precious a thing to permit its devaluation by living pointlessly, emptily, without love, and finally, without hope" (1993:68).

My hope is that this book has provided you insights and strategies to support you in your fight for what is right, just, and reasonable as you stretch others and yourself to a higher level in the face of adversity.

EPILOGUE:
A NATIONAL CALL TO ACTION

After completing my final review of the manuscript before sending it to the publisher, I had a disturbing feeling of unfinished business. I agonized over the feeling for quite a period of time, reluctant to let go of the manuscript until I solved the mystery of my disturbance. Then it dawned on me. This book is filled with lessons about how to think and act to lead your organization to a new level. But you are saddled with the responsibility of figuring out how to get the professional development training you need, particularly as it relates to your leading specific change initiatives, to make the leadership lessons have direct payoff to you in your environment. In other words, I write in the book about your providing support, information, and resources to help others become resilient in the face of adversity. At the same time, most educational leaders do not have a ready source of ongoing, embedded professional development training available in the areas of organizational change, effective leadership of culture change, and resilience. Sure, there are one-time conferences and workshops but nothing on a national scale that is systemic.

Another epiphany I had in my struggle to make sense of the "disturbing feeling" is that the national leadership organizations could play a major leadership role in helping to fill this gap. So I have taken the risk to write the following letter to each of the major educational leadership organizations. The intent of the letter is to generate public dialogue and debate, a National Call to Action, about how the national leadership organizations can take a leading role in responding nationally to two questions posed in the letter.

I do not know, as I write this epilogue, where this call to action will go, if anywhere. I feel less disturbed, however, having put the issue on the table about the gap I see between what we know are important skills in leading organizations in the specific area of *culture change* and what we are doing about it on a national scale.

My hope is that we find ways to close the gap. You, your colleagues, and the students will benefit.

• • •

Dear (National Organization):

In 1997 I authored a book published by the American Association of School Administrators called *Coming Clean about Organizational Change.* As I am completing a revised edition, *Coming Even Cleaner about Organizational Change,* I am more struck than ever by an overpowering conclusion. Throughout the United States, private publishers and leadership organizations such as yours offer products and services of the highest quality that have significant promise for bringing about changes in teaching and learning. In other words, the products and services *could have* a profound effect on culture change in schools.

I emphasize *could have* because it is not happening on a broad scale. Based on five decades of work by serious scholars of organizational change, the results are conclusive: rarely are any culture change initiatives actually implemented for at least six years in any educational culture.

This is where your organization and other national educational leadership organizations have an unfulfilled obligation. With the best of intentions, you are providing products and services that *could have* major culture change impact on what happens in schools. The harsh reality is that the national organizations are not doing enough systemically in the way of ongoing, embedded leadership development training to help increase the odds that the intended culture change will ever happen.

This letter is a National Call to Action. I call upon your organization and your fellow national educational leadership organizations to convene a Culture Change Summit to address these basic questions: "How can we as national educational leadership organizations create ongoing dialogue and action that lead to *systemic* training to help school leaders achieve the intended culture changes we champion? How can we provide this training so that it directly connects to school leaders' implementation of the products and services we provide?"

My remarks are not meant as a criticism of past practice. This is a plea for the future. One national educational organization offers almost 1,000 products and services to schools or school districts. Districts nationwide are investing hundreds of millions of dollars in hopes of a return on their investment. Yet one thing "we already know but don't want to talk about" is that this investment is not paying off in terms of culture change.

The prestige and influence of your organization can play a prominent role in responding to this National Call to Action. I look forward to your organization's positive response.

Sincerely,
Jerry L. Patterson

REFERENCES

Argyris, C. 1999. *On Organizational Learning.* 2d ed. Malden, Mass.: Blackwell.

Barth, R. 2002. The Culture Builder. *Educational Leadership* 59(10): 6–11.

Block, P. 1987. *The Empowered Manager: Positive Political Skills at Work.* San Francisco: Jossey-Bass.

Bolman, L. G., and T. E. Deal. 1997. *Reframing Organizations: Artistry, Choice, and Leadership.* 2d ed. San Francisco: Jossey-Bass.

Bridges, W. 1991. *Managing Transitions.* Reading, Mass.: Addison-Wesley.

Cameron, K. S., and R. E. Quinn. 1999. *Diagnosing and Changing Organizational Culture.* Reading, Mass.: Addison-Wesley.

Collins, J. 2001. Level 5 Leadership: The Triumph of Humility and Fierce Resolve. *Harvard Business Review* 79(2): 67–73.

Collins, J., and J. Porras. 1994. *Built to Last.* New York: HarperCollins.

Conner, D. 1992. *Managing at the Speed of Change.* New York: Villard Books.

Cooper, B., L. Fusarelli, and V. Carella. 2000. *Career Crisis in the Superintendency? The Results of a National Survey.* Arlington, Va.: American Association of School Administrators.

Farson, R. 1996. *Management of the Absurd: Paradoxes in Leadership.* New York: Simon and Schuster.

Fisher, R., and S. Brown. 1988. *Getting Together: Building a Relationship That Gets to YES.* Boston: Houghton Mifflin.

Froiland, P. 1993. What Cures Job Stress? *Training* 30(12): 32–36.

Fullan, M. 1991. *The New Meaning of Educational Change.* New York: Teachers College Press.

———. 1998. Breaking the Bonds of Dependency. *Educational Leadership* 58(9): 6–10.

———. 2002. The Change Leader. *Educational Leadership* 59(10): 16–20

Fullan, M., and N. Watson. 1991. Beyond School-University Partnerships. In *Teacher Development and Educational Change.* Edited by M. Fullan and A. Hargreaves. East Sussex, U.K.: Falmer Press.

Gerstner, L., Jr. 2002. *Who Says Elephants Can't Dance? Inside IBM's Historic Turnaround.* New York: Harper Business.

Giuliani, R. 2002. *Leadership.* New York: Miramax Books.

Glickman, C. D. 2002. The Courage to Lead. *Educational Leadership* 59(10): 41–44.

Goldberg, M. F. 2000a. Leadership for Change: An Interview with John Goodlad. *Phi Delta Kappan* 82(1): 82–85.

———. 2000b. *Profiles of Leadership in Education.* Bloomington, Ind.: Phi Delta Kappa Educational Foundation.

———. 2001. Leadership in Education: Five Commonalities. *Phi Delta Kappan* 82(10): 757–61.

Goodlad, J. 1984. *A Place Called School.* New York: McGraw-Hill.

Hall, G., and S. Hord. 2001. *Implementing Change: Patterns, Principles, and Potholes.* Boston: Allyn and Bacon.

Hall, G., and S. Loucks. 1978. *Innovation Configurations: Analyzing the Adaptations of Innovations.* Report No. 3049. Austin: University of Texas at Austin, Research and Development Center in Teacher Education.

Havel, V. 1993. Never Hope against Hope. *Esquire* 121(4): 68.

Heifetz, R., and D. Laurie. 1997. The Work of Leadership. *Harvard Business Review* 75: 124–34.

Heifetz, R., and M. Linsky. 2002a. A Survival Guide for Leaders. *Harvard Business Review* 80(6): 65–74.

———. 2002b. *Leadership on the Line: Staying Alive through the Dangers of Leading.* Boston: Harvard Business School Press.

Hesselbein, F. 2002. *Hesselbein on Leadership.* San Francisco: Jossey-Bass.

Ibarra, H. 2002. How to Stay Stuck in the Wrong Career. *Harvard Business Review* 80(12): 40–47.

Johnson, J. 2002. Staying Ahead of the Game. *Educational Leadership* 59(10): 26–30.

Johnson, S. 1998. *Who Moved My Cheese?* New York: G. P. Putnam's Sons.

Kaner, S. 1996. *Facilitator's Guide to Participatory Decision-Making.* Gabriola Island, B.C.: New Society Publishers/Canada.

Kanter, R. M. 1999. The Enduring Skills of Change Leaders. *Leader to Leader* (13): 15–22.

Kanter, R. M., B. A. Stein, and T. D. Jick. 1992. *The Challenge of Organizational Change: How Companies Experience It and Leaders Guide It.* New York: The Free Press.

Kotter, J. P. 1996. *Leading Change.* Boston: Harvard Business School Press.

———. 2001. "What Leaders Really Do." *Harvard Business Review* 79(112): 85–96.

———. 2002. *The Heart of Change.* Boston: Harvard Business School Press.

Lencioni, P. M. 2002. Make Your Values Mean Something. *Harvard Business Review* 80(7): 113–17.

Lieberman, A. 1992. School/University Collaboration: A View from the Inside. *Phi Delta Kappan* 74: 147–55.

Muncey, D., and P. McQuillan. 1993. Preliminary Findings from a Five-Year Study of the Coalition of Essential Schools. *Phi Delta Kappan* 74(6): 486–89.

O'Reilly, C., and J. Pfeffer. 2000. *Hidden Value: How Great Companies Achieve Extraordinary Results with Ordinary People.* Boston: Harvard Business School Press.

Oshry, B. 1992. *The Possibilities of Organization.* Boston: Power and Systems.

O'Toole, J. 1995. *Leading Change.* San Francisco: Jossey-Bass.

Patterson, J. 1997. *Coming Clean about Organizational Change.* Arlington, Va.: American Association of School Administrators.

Patterson, J. 2000. *The Anguish of Leadership.* Arlington, Va.: American Association of School Administrators.

Patterson, J., and J. Patterson. 2001. Resilience in the Face of Imposed Changes. *Principal Leadership* 1(6): 50–55.

Patterson, J., J. Patterson, and L. Collins. 2002. *Bouncing Back! How Your School Can Succeed in the Face of Adversity.* Larchmont, N.Y.: Eye On Education.

Patterson, J., S. Purkey, and J. Parker. 1986. *Productive School Systems for a Nonrational World.* Alexandria, Va.: Association for Supervision and Curriculum Development.

Ross, M., M. Green, and C. Henderson. 1993. *The American College President.* Washington, D.C.: American Council on Education.

Sarason, S. 1996. *Revisiting the Culture of the School and the Problem of Change.* New York: Teachers College Press.

Schein, E. H. 1999a. Empowerment, Coercive Persuasion and Organizational Learning: Do They Connect? *The Learning Organization* 6(4): 163–72.

———. 1999b. *The Corporate Culture Survival Guide.* San Francisco: Jossey-Bass.

Schlechty, P. C. 1993. On the Frontier of School Reform with Trailblazers, Pioneers and Settlers. *Journal of Staff Development* 14: 46–51.

Tichy, N., and R. Charan. 1995. The CEO as Coach: An Interview with Allied
    Signal's Lawrence A. Bossidy. *Harvard Business Review* 73: 69–78.
Yee, G., and L. Cuban. 1996. When Is Tenure Long Enough? A Historical
    Analysis of Superintendent Turnover in Urban School Districts. *Educational
    Administration Quarterly* 32(4): 615–41.

INDEX

action plan, 26, 76, 77, 98
adversity, vii, 1, 7–9; ongoing vs.
    crisis, 10–12
anatomy of leadership pain, 105–8
"and" thinking, viii, 35, 96, 111
anguish of leadership, 107–8
anticipation of disruptions, 114–15
architects vs. victims, 30, 50–51, 88;
    leadership implications, 52–55
autonomy, 50–51

best-case outcomes, 69, 112–13
burden of proof, 38, 44–45

caring, 8, 16, 75–81,101–2, 117–18
choice, 101, 103, 117–18
clarity, 101–2, 117–18
climate of caring and support, 95;
    leadership strategies, 95–97
coercive persuasion, 68
communication, 37–39
compliance change, 4

conflict in organizations, 81–83, 88;
    leadership implications, 83–84
consensus building, 84
core value package, 75
core values, 73–76, 80–81, 88; core
    educational values, 74; ethics, 73;
    hierarchy, 73; specific educational
    initiatives, 74
courage of convictions, 110–11;
    leadership strategies, 111–13
culture change, 2–3

damage control, 42
decision making, 58–59, 62
denial of harsh realities, 84–88
dependency, 51
disruptions to expectations, 113

effective leadership, 5–7
"either/or" thinking, 35, 110
endings and loss, 98, 102–3;
    leadership strategies, 98–100